FROM IDEA TO REALITY: A YOUNG ADULT'S GUIDE TO ENTREPRENEURSHIP & SUCCESS

7 PRINCIPLES OF PROSPERITY, PAVING THE PATH TO FINANCIAL FREEDOM FOR THE YOUNG ENTREPRENEUR

MICHAEL J. THORNTON

STERLING
PUBLICATIONS

STERLING

PUBLICATIONS

CONTENTS

Part III
TAKING YOUR WEALTH TO THE
NEXT LEVEL

INTRODUCTION

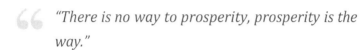 *"There is no way to prosperity, prosperity is the way."*

— WAYNE DYER

Welcome to the realm of personal finance, wealth creation, and entrepreneurship. We live in a world where life is inherently uncertain, and a global pandemic or a major event can serve as a stark reminder of the fragility of our financial stability. In such times, it is of the utmost importance to possess a thorough understanding of the mechanics of money and the strategies for wealth creation.

This book is intended to provide young adults with a comprehensive guide to navigating the intricacies of personal finance and entrepreneurship. By equipping readers with the knowledge and tools necessary for financial autonomy and goal attainment, this book aims to empower individuals to take charge of their financial futures.

Drawing on current research in the fields of behavioral economics and finance, this book employs a unique, narrative-driven approach to imparting financial literacy and entrepreneurial principles. From analyzing the psychological underpinnings of spending habits to delving into the intricacies of starting and growing a business, this book aims to furnish readers with the knowledge and strategies required to succeed in the modern economy.

It is a fact that many individuals are living paycheck to paycheck, and being trapped in a job that is unfulfilling, solely for the purpose of meeting financial obligations, can be an arduous experience. Waking up each morning to engage in activities that do not align with one's passions is a waste of one's potential.

In this light, when renowned investor Warren Buffett was given the opportunity to address high school students in his hometown, he offered a single piece of financial advice before taking questions. He advised the students to "avoid credit cards" as a means of avoiding financial pitfalls. This advice from Buffett is prudent and following it will ensure that one does not fall victim to financial missteps.

Whether you are just embarking on your financial journey or seeking to take your wealth-building efforts to the next level, this book serves as an indispensable guide for anyone seeking to comprehend the nuances of personal finance and create a brighter future for themselves and their loved ones.

Why Should You Read This Book?

If you're holding this book, it is clear you are someone who is not content just to sit around and dwell in the realm of mediocrity. Rather you recognise your future is out there, but you just need some guidance on how to realise your potential. Maybe you're tired of your current job or you're a young person looking to take control of your financial future. Maybe you're just looking for some ways to be more financially stable as you plan for retirement. Whatever your situation is, you've come to the right place.

This book contains a wealth of information that can help you on your way to realising this dream. Helping people achieve their financial goals is something I am passionate about having seen what it is like to be 'on the other side' and having made all the mistakes myself. As a striving entrepreneur, mentor, and financial advisor,

I've seen my fair share of people who are struggling with their finances, and I understand what it's like to be in that position and yet have no certainty of where to go.

As you delve deeper into the contents of this book, you'll learn, not only about the ins and outs of starting your own business, but you'll also gain a more comprehensive understanding of the true essence of prosperity. On top of this, I've included some tips and strategies along the way for taking advantage of tax benefits for entrepreneurs and other nuggets of wisdom for the aspiring entrepreneur, so if that's something that interests you, you're going to love this book. At the end of the day, who wouldn't want a guide to becoming financially stable and secure?

ABOUT THE AUTHOR

Michael Thornton: a visionary entrepreneur, dedicated mentor, and passionate advocate for empowering the youth. My story is one of humble beginnings, relentless determination, and hard-earned success. Raised in a small, blue-collar town, our family of nine shared a tiny 3-bedroom home. My upbringing taught me the values of diligence, perseverance, and hard work. Armed with this knowledge I set out to try and build ourselves a better future.

Lacking guidance, my journey took a winding route. Initially, I served in the military for a few years. Afterward, I sought to reintegrate into civilian life, obtaining a degree in Economics, believing it would be my springboard to success and a fulfilling career. Yet, merely two years into my first job at a bank, I realized this path wasn't meant for me.

My entrepreneurial journey had actually began at 19 with odd jobs and a relentless pursuit of knowledge. I fixed computers, worked as a tutor, and bought and sold curios, all while honing my skills and building my experiences. I stumbled often, made even more mistakes, and faced numerous setbacks, but with each challenge, my growth and determination only grew, and I became the wiser for it.

With each new endeavor, I learned more about the intricacies of business, finance and personal development. My initial failures became the bedrock of my success, as I used them
Over time, I built a legacy of thriving businesses, building on my roots, founding a chain of education centres, as well as diversifying into general commerce, tech, and property. These ventures have not only brought me financial gain but also allowed me to help many people unlock their potential and achieve their goals.

Today, as a mentor and serial entrepreneur, I am privileged to guide young adults on their journey toward self-discovery and success. I share my experiences and wisdom, giving people the guidance, I never had, helping them learn from mistakes they never need make.

In this book I invite you to embark on a journey with me, where we will explore the depths of your potential, confront your fears, and forge an unbreakable connection with your inner strength. Together, we will chart a course toward a future that is not only financially secure but also rich in purpose and joy.

PART I

THE MINDSET OF PROSPERITY

STERLING
PUBLICATIONS

1

THE SECRET OF PROSPERITY

W ealth. Abundance. Money. Prosperity. Success. Whatever you choose to name it, whatever it means to you, we all want these things. Whether it is to live the lifestyle you desire, to accomplish things you have always wanted to do, or just to have peace of mind, wealth is vital. However, I genuinely believe that the secret to riches is our attitude about it. Do you feel peaceful and joyful when you think about money and prosperity, or are you nervous and overwhelmed? When we consider what we want in life, it is critical to feel good about it right now, and to feel as if we already have it.

True prosperity comes from being able to meet your mental, spiritual, and bodily requirements. There is, however, a significant gap between what you require and what you desire. True prosperity entails having at your disposal the items needed for survival. Unfortunately, very few individuals comprehend what is required, or even understand the true meaning of the word "needs." If your demands are narrowed down to a few particular items, the need can be readily met.

For an individual to be successful in life, they must be driven by a purpose. Most individuals devote their entire lives and energies to making money, and some successful people even die of heart failure just when they are about to find happiness. If you have a lot of money, but have a lot of problems with everyone, you have very little. When happiness eludes you, the entire purpose of life becomes meaningless. When wealth is lost, you have just suffered a little setback. When you lose your health, you also lose something else, but when your peace of mind is gone, everything is gone.

Money is not a misfortune. It is vital to consider how you spend your money. If you ask a dollar bill, "Shall I purchase poison with you?" it does not respond. However, if you abuse this dollar bill, you will be unhappy, and it will bring you delight when used correctly.

No saint or genius does not employ money in their activity. Whoever eats must pay for the food, and it is preferable to be able to buy your food than rely on charity. There is worth in everything.

It is critical to understand how to become rich. True prosperity comes from improving your mental efficiency, which allows you to supply the things you require. If you know how to divert your attention away from all distractions and focus it on one object of concentration, you will be able to attract what you require. After you have found the answers to all of your questions within yourself, you will be able to declare "I am prosperous."

Prosperity is the comprehensive version of your wealth and can be viewed as wealth on steroids. This means that visualizing prosperity will encompass the wealth platforms. You will have enough money and assets to provide you with financial stability, and those funds and assets are set up in platforms that drive them to continuously create additional money and assets.

You are now in a position where you wake up every day wealthier than when you went to bed the night before. You are suddenly a rich man. However, being rich does not imply being prosperous. You must now take those riches and combine them with other subtle aspects of prosperity, such as:

- Spiritual anchoring
- Vibrant health
- Self-esteem
- Relationship empowerment
- Work or a mission that provides you with challenges and opportunities to learn

This brings you to the "sweet spot," where you are grateful for everything you do, have, and become while still having the drive, desire, and ability to do, have, and become even more. That is a successful way of life.

MEASURES OF SUCCESS

Do you consider yourself successful? Do people tell you that you are successful? If you could actually find a means to quantify actual success, you may be able to convince yourself that you have made it. This is frequently how an entrepreneur thinks. I want to be successful and make my company ideas a reality, and because I am an optimistic person, I see myself as successful. However, my stakeholders in the firm want to see a metric that proves it is truly successful.

Starting with some fundamental measures and concluding with some more unusual ways to look about success metrics, here are seven ways you may evaluate how successful you and your business are becoming:

The Profitability

It is relatively obvious that when your firm makes money, it indicates some level of success, especially if there is money left over after all expenditures have been met. You may have even reached a tipping point after months of being in the red. However, being in the black for a year or more will be your actual measure of success. From there, your ultimate measure of success will be the creation of long-term profitability.

This may include strategic changes, as well as regular assessments of your processes and expenses to see where you can become leaner and more efficient. I recall those first few months when I finally had enough money to pay myself, which is when I realized I was finally getting somewhere.

Number of Clients

Every business needs a client. I have never reached the point where I have concluded I have had enough customers. Your success should be demonstrated by a rising client base and a continuous flow of prospects in the pipeline. Those pioneering clients were thrilling to me, but as I started to see more and more people express an interest in and buy what I was selling, I realized I had made a good decision, and that countless hours of study and promotion had finally paid off.

However, that actual measure of success in terms of client count was just transitory. To attract more of my target audience, I needed to keep working harder and smarter.

Customers' Levels of Satisfaction

Beyond the number of clients, my ultimate measure of success was how satisfied I made the ones I did have. Word of mouth is an incredibly powerful tool in business, so their happiness would imply that future clients will be influenced by what they said to their friends, family, and colleagues, rather than by my research and marketing. The ability to please my clients meant that everything I had learned about them, and their requirements was being appropriately applied to the service I was providing them. It is also critical to develop customer service rules for your firm, so that everyone who works there understands their role in meeting the demands of consumers. It just takes one poor customer experience to derail the successful and happy customer service experience you have built up.

Employee Contentment

Employees that are happy and motivated may tell you a lot about your true success, as their productivity is the motor that drives the company forward. If an employee is both satisfied with their job and a naturally hard worker, then their work becomes both higher-effort and more efficient. Additionally, positively minded staff can convey the same feelings to your clientele; when staff smile at customers, the customer also feels pleased, and they become aware that your company is a well-meaning and productive one. When each employee goes above and beyond their job description, the company thrives. In my own business, I have focused on establishing a pleasant work environment that provides employees with everything they need to accomplish their tasks, while also working to ensure that my staff enjoys their work while doing it.

I have also made sure that my remote employees are happy with the work they are doing, and I frequently tell them how much I appreciate their efforts. If an employee is placed in a position like this that makes them feel cast off from the rest of your company, it is important to help them feel like they are a part of the whole team, and that they are not alone. When they have questions, I make myself available, so they do not feel irritated due to a lack of communication. A happy business has happy employees, which ultimately makes it a successful business.

Self-Satisfaction

I have learned through the years that someone can be content in life while still having the desire to pursue new projects and interests. It has been a valuable lesson for me to recognize the importance of feeling happy with the results of a business as it grows and celebrating those "wins" along the road. I enjoy working, but it took some time to figure out how to combine that contentment with achievements with my burning desire to accomplish more.

Learning and Knowledge Level

While this may appear to be an unusual approach to evaluate success, it is actually rather important to an entrepreneur, given that it is this learning and information that provides you with the market, customer, competition, and economic data to assist build your strategy. This ongoing learning is derived not only from what I have studied or observed, but also from experience obtained by implementing my plan and observing the results. In the end, failure is required to acquire a particular level of learning and understanding, so running from it is ill-advised.

Throughout my career, learning from my mistakes has become an essential component of reaching true success. As I progress forward, I know what has tripped me up in the past, so I have the ability to avoid the potholes and speed bumps that can impede progress. The entire process of learning these pitfalls reminds me of the phrase "street smarts," since you have to learn them while getting into the thick of the action instead of while sitting on the couch watching television.

What You Do with Your Free Time

Determining how you spend your time each day is a true measure of success, since it shows you if you have been able to delegate, establish an efficient organization, and defines what your key goals should be as a company leader. I work constantly, but I discovered that I might be more productive by prioritizing duties and delegating some of the less critical ones. I was able to let others take the lead, which helped them develop into a wonderful, trusted team.

The most significant advantage of this, however, was that it freed up time for me to focus on those key areas in which I excelled. This assisted me in providing a clearer direction for the firm, and also provided me with time for introspection and personal growth and the ability to carve out more personal time to care for myself and spend time with family and friends.

As you can see, the majority of these genuine indicators of success are qualitative, rather than quantitative amounts concerning your financial reports and bottom line. Each of these measures needs ongoing attention, and they impact the outcomes of the other ideas on the list. If I am dissatisfied, my staff will most certainly be dissatisfied as well. If consumers are unsatisfied, it is possible that they are the victims of a disgruntled employee, or that a disgruntled customer is pointing to our lack of understanding of what they require.

The true measure of success, then, is to deliver on all seven of these acts at the same time for yourself, your workers, and your organization, both now and in the future.

THE TRUE MEASURE OF PROSPERITY

There are many ways to measure the notion of prosperity, and each criterion may work better for different demographics of people. In this section, we will analyze and discuss many of the ways you may quantify this success.

Wealth

Let's start with the obvious quality. When you have prosperity, it means you have accumulated a certain wealth that can keep you comfortable for long periods. Some people measure their prosperity by this very point, hoping to make enough money so that they do not have to work another day in their life.

To quantify prosperity, most economists have typically used a basic economic metric known as gross domestic product, or GDP. GDP is the most known and commonly used metric of national progress, whether measured in total for a country or per capita. As it encompasses the value of all products in the economy, whether consumed by individuals, governments, or businesses, it is an exceptionally valuable single indicator of a country's well-being.

Household gross disposable income is a highly appealing indicator of a country's inhabitants' material living conditions. It acts as the total of salaries, interest and other financial returns, property income, net financial transfers, the value of government-provided services such as healthcare and education, and other products and services supplied by non-profit organizations, subtracting any taxes paid to the government.

Household income per capita, again neglecting distributional factors, estimates how much the average household can consume. Household income reflects prosperity to the extent that prosperity is dependent on market products and services, as well as government and non-profit services.

This emphasis on commodities and services when attempting to evaluate wealth may appear to be limiting at first glance, but there are plenty of other ways to analyze income and monetary value that may work out in the event that this method does not.

Debt

Another way to measure your prosperity is by checking if you are debt-free. Debt is a struggle for so many people, and it can limit how much money you make, how much you move up in the world, and how happy you can become. Larger debts can limit what you want to do, and how quickly you can reach your desired prosperity.

Understanding how debt restricts your financial options and how a variety of techniques may assist you can assist you in controlling, reducing, and eliminating it. If you are attempting to find out how to manage your obligations, establish a list of how much you owe and to which suppliers, as well as how much you pay in fees and interest to each. While this may be an unpleasant wake-up call, it will provide you with a clear picture of where you are, and how varying interest rates and fees may influence the amount you pay back.

Aside from determining exactly what you owe, it may also be beneficial to understand how much money you have coming in, how much cash is necessary for the necessities, and where the remainder of your money may be going. This will assist you in determining where there may be room for movement, and where you may be able to extract a little extra to contribute to your repayments. Time management and debt management frequently go hand-in-hand, since paying bills on time may help you avoid things like late penalties and interest costs.

Remember that late payments might result in black marks on your credit report, which can impair your ability to borrow money because it shows lenders if you have been paying on time.

Sustainability

When we say sustainability, it means you have enough wealth, income, assets, and materials to keep you existing. For example, millionaires have enough money to sustain their lives for very long periods, if not forever.

Sustainability focuses on satisfying the demands of the present without jeopardizing future generations' capacity to meet their own needs. Sustainability is built on the economic, environmental, and social pillars, also known commonly as profits, planet, and people. Companies are increasingly making public pledges to sustainability through decreasing waste, investing in renewable energy, and supporting groups that strive toward a more sustainable future.

When you are sustained financially, you have no worries about prospering as an individual.

A Warren Buffett Contrast

Warren Buffett is not surprised that wealth is the key to determining whether economic progress over time is sustainable. Many consider him to be the most successful investor of our time, not only because his net worth is present at $45 billion, but also because he began in 1950 with only $100,000 (adjusting for 2015 inflation) and consistently invested in firms that increased in value fast (Mumford, 2016). How did Buffett choose the firms he believed would provide the biggest profits in the future?

Assume that while analyzing a firm, Buffett only has access to the income statements, which show annual sales and costs. He would know how much money the firm generated from sales in each period, as well as how much money the company spent on labor, supplies, and acquiring assets. The difference between total revenue and total expenditure, which is known as the company's profits or bottom line, is reported at the bottom of the income statement for each period. Companies that have had profit growth may likewise experience future profit growth. It would be straightforward for Buffett to rank all firms based on profit growth and then invest solely in those with the highest growth rate.

The problem with this method is that there is no way to distinguish between two firms with the same profit growth rates if one is significantly investing in future income-producing initiatives while the other is selling off assets. The income figures alone would not make a difference. As a result, Buffett examines the company's balance sheet, which shows the worth of all assets and liabilities in each quarter. He then invests in firms whose net worth has risen by investing in new assets with a high potential for future profit, even if present earnings are modest. These current investments will eventually generate future rewards.

2

THE MILLIONAIRE MINDSET

L ook at what is possible, as opposed to what is not possible, in order to develop a Prosperity Mindset. Abundance declares that there are plenty of resources, and it believes that anything is ideal. It fosters happiness and acceptance, allowing one to recognize the worth and usefulness of what is. In contrast, scarcity focuses on what we do not have and the fact that there is not enough of it. It instils a sense of fear and causes a panic to take or obtain these resources, because there will not be enough, or you may not have enough. It is normal for us to perceive the universe and life from a sacristy perspective because of our inherently bad human wiring.

For example, two kids are sharing a toy and think to themselves, "If I don't get the toy I want now, I might not get it later." As an adult, if you do not obtain the job you apply for, you have scarcity concerns, such as "I will not get a job or did poorly." The distinction is that an abundance mindset, which shares certain parallels or overlaps with the growth mindset, views things differently. Abundance knows I will play with the toy at some point, and that if I keep trying, I will find the perfect job at the right moment. To me, the difference between abundance and scarcity is a matter of faith against fear.

Attachment is a method of seeing, thinking, and doing which is usually connected to my own method. I have a predetermined notion of how things should go and appear, and if it does not go that way, I consider it a failure. On the other hand, unattachment is the ability to let go of something and trust that if it is meant to be, it will return. Unattachment has objectives and visions, yet it is open to how things may grow or unfold. That does not imply going off course or in ten different ways; rather, it means being open to possibilities and opportunities as they present themselves and being flexible enough to identify them, even if they are not what you expected.

For example, suppose you apply for a job at Apple but do not get it. You are offered the option to volunteer at the high school and assist with the tech club, which would allow you to accomplish something related to your goal and make contacts that would help you achieve it in the future. Possibilities that present themselves like this are often much better than we can envision. Think about it like this:

Growth Mindset + Prosperity Perspective + Unattachment (what can I learn and grow + what is possible and what can I accomplish + open to whatever happens without rules, limitations, or demands on how that unfolds) = Prosperity Thinking.

This mentality will motivate you to attain happiness and maintain a high quality of life, regardless of whether you are wealthy or not. In a way, it is a form of self-love and empowerment, helping you have the liveliness and energy to achieve greatness when you have a prosperity mentality. To have a successful mentality, you must have the desire to improve yourself because you like yourself and want to see yourself reach amazing heights. You are empowering yourself, challenging yourself, and teaching yourself how to live a prosperous and long-lasting life.

It all begins with your attitude. A wealthy mentality is high-vibrational energy that attracts new situations, people, and events into your life to assist you in creating it. A mentality is a collection of beliefs or a style of thinking that shapes one's actions, worldview, and mental attitude. This mentality produces feelings, which are energy that is released into the Universal Field, attracting additional possibilities to experience more of what you are experiencing and seeking.

CULTIVATING A PROSPERITY MINDSET

> *"Prosperity is the experience of having plenty of what we truly need and want in life, material and otherwise."*

> — SHAKTI GAWAIN

When I assist people in being more aware of their finances and understanding their money beliefs, I am assisting them in learning to use money as a tool. Being wealthy and successful entails more than just having a lot of money, but also developing a wealthy mentality. To me, this mentality is being able to do everything you want without being constrained by financial constraints, but it also encompasses much more, such as being thankful for what we have in our lives daily.

Prosperity is a form of liberty. It is an internal mindset and a way of life. However, it is about so much more than money, being a feeling of abundance in all aspects of our lives. "How can I take care of my physical requirements in this material world?" you might wonder. We all know that we need to work to provide for our bodily necessities, desires, and to preserve for the future. When you simply think about money and the material world, though, you will always be on the hamster wheel of never having enough.

What fascinates me is that even those who have a lot of money feel compelled to acquire more or risk losing what they have. They cling to the money as if it were a lifeline. More often than not, the more money you earn, the more you spend. No matter how much money you have, it is a black hole of "I need more money." Even people who make a lot of money or come into a lot of money have anxiety.

Being prosperous is a state of mind, a style of thinking and doing that acts as your inner universe of beliefs and thoughts. The fact that someone is financially successful does not imply that they are happy. Your financial situation does not ensure success; you can be happy even if you do not have a lot of money, and it is critical to be grateful for what you do have and how they care for your needs. Feeling prosperous does not imply that you have a lot, or that you require further resources.

I want you to learn how to believe that you are already wealthy. I also advise you to become aware of any childhood beliefs that are preventing you from achieving your goals.

What you wanted last year is not the same as what you desire now. Following your heart's desires will bring you prosperity and happiness. Being in nature, surrounded by natural beauty, makes me feel fortunate. If you grew up with an attitude of poverty and did not have a lot of money or possessions, your vision of the world may constantly feel like there is not enough. You can feel wealthy even if you do not have a lot of money, and you might feel impoverished even if you have a lot of wealth. The goal is to have a positive mentality.

Every one of us has beliefs and behaviors that prevent us from living the life we desire. Many of these ideas are built into our operating system, and were instilled in us by our parents when we were young. We did not always get our fundamental needs addressed, such as affection, attention, adequate food, or appropriate clothing, and as a result, we had a specific way of seeing life without these needs. The key to waking up and co-creating the life you desire is becoming mindful of what you believe. You can identify what is preventing you from enjoying a happy and successful life.

Follow Your Heart's Desire to Truly be Prosperous

You must question what it is you want as often as possible. What are the things that are most important to me in life? What are some of my wants and needs that I would want to have met? Remember to connect your wants and needs with your heart's desire. I urge you to experience feeling prosperous by following the upcoming advice:

Gratitude: The Key to Happiness

I propose writing down what you are grateful for each day in a stream-of-consciousness manner. Another method to accomplish this is to state out loud what you are grateful for when you wake up and before you move around to get up. Keep a notebook on hand to record all of the positive things that occur in your life. When you look at this list as a whole, you will see how much good is going on in your life.

How Do You Define a Wealthy Life?

It is important to remember that it is not only about money and the tangible world. What would your emotional, mental, physical, and spiritual lives be like if you were genuinely wealthy?

SCARCITY MINDSET KEEPS YOU STUCK

Our attitude toward plenitude or scarcity has a tremendous impact on our lives and determines our daily actions. There is a significant distinction between these two words which divides happy people from sad people, and it is easy to alter it to pick the bright side. Because you keep seeking more and more when you have a mindset of wealth and plenty, it might influence where you go in life. It assists you in living your life by instructing you on how to live it, and even goes into detail on how you may strive to increase your success, wealth, and long-term viability. Instead of a life of sadness, worry, and tension, an abundant mentality may lead to pleasure and fulfillment.

Scarcity, on the other hand, keeps you stuck and prevents you from going forward. If you have a scarcity mindset, you feel there is not enough to succeed, giving you a nagging feeling that you will never have enough money to live a free, happy, and fulfilled life. Because you have to worry about your next paycheck, a scarcity mindset may imprison you in a life of dread, which is not joyful in a life of affluence.

The next issue is: how can we move from a scarcity attitude to one of abundance?

Focus on What You Currently Have

If you have been considering a career shift, but have not yet taken the plunge, you are probably thinking things like, "There are not enough decent jobs out there," or "There are not enough excellent jobs out there." "Who am I kidding, there is too much competition," or "I do not have enough transferrable abilities." All of these concepts are founded on scarcity, or what you do not have. A scarcity mindset sees limitations rather than possibilities. Instead, think positive thoughts such as, "Wow, I have 25 years of marketing expertise, which will be a tremendous advantage if I decide to start a business," or "Over the previous 10 years, I have developed fantastic contacts, which will be crucial when I start networking for my next job."

Make Win-Win Circumstances

According to a scarcity mindset, if one person succeeds, another loses. To fight this way of thinking, try to create win-win situations in your life. Look for methods for both sides to feel accomplished and better about the connection at the end of the meeting. Consider putting this into practice in both your personal and professional lives.

Develop the Ability to Detect Possibilities

According to an interesting Harvard experiment conducted in 2020, when we focus extremely intensely on one thing, other options that are there in front of us might go entirely undetected. Because the brain can only receive so much information at once, if you believe that "I cannot do it" or "it is impossible," all other ideas that contradict that belief will be discarded (Castrillon, 2020). As such, you should begin to teach your mind to shift its attention and build a broader sense of awareness. You may see more possibilities, choices, and resources in your life when you have an abundant mindset.

SHIFTING FROM SCARCITY TO PROSPERITY

It is not difficult to go from a scarcity mindset to a prosperity attitude, even if you are locked in one. Going through this transition may give you the strength, confidence, bravery, and optimism you need to achieve some of your life's largest goals. If you are unable to make the necessary changes, you may find yourself stranded and wondering what may have been.

Some folks yearn for these things and spend much of their time fantasizing about them, but few take the effort to define what these three things mean to them. If you do not know what plentiful, successful, or rich looks like for you, how can you become more abundant, prosperous, or wealthy?

Each of them may be experienced differently, so I have put up a helpful summary to help you distinguish between them. It will be a lot simpler to educate your mind to think abundantly, helping you feel affluent at all times, once you know which is which and can recognize which mentality you are now in.

DEFINING WEALTH AND ABUNDANCE

Wealth

For some people, having a specific amount in their bank account may be sufficient to count for wealthiness. Other people, however, may believe it means reaching the point where they would never have to worry about money again. The key thing to remember is that money is only a means of obtaining the 'things' you desire, so let me ask you this question: Do you know what you want?

One excellent approach to describe this is to ask yourself, "What would I do or acquire if I had limitless wealth?" What would it take for me to tell myself, "I am now affluent" or "I am now wealthy"? We tend to lose sight of why we desire more money in the first place; you may believe you want more money, but what matters is what you will be able to accomplish with it if you have a lot of it. In other cases, we may believe that we require a certain amount of money to be genuinely successful.

Prosperity

Even though by definition, this term indicates joy, honesty, success, and serenity, it is also a state of mind. Prosperity is the whole emotional package, not just a slew of worldly possessions. Achieving and sustaining a high quality of life is essential to living a wealthy life or having a prosperous attitude.

Abundance

This attitude is founded on the assumption that there is plenty of everything for everyone. All that is necessary is the ability to perceive things as they are, rather than through the lens of a sense of scarcity. Having an abundance mentality rather than a scarcity mindset may be a deciding factor in how you live and manage your life.

This might completely transform your life, because what you think to be true frequently becomes your reality. More pleasure, contentment, and less connection to negative emotions like sadness, anger, and fear are frequently associated with an abundant mentality.

PART II

BUILDING A STRONG FOUNDATION

3

FOCUS ON CLARITY

W hen you think with clarity, you are exposing your mind to a world of possibilities and noticing things you would not have noticed before. Imagine you are on top of a mountain, gazing down into the valley, with a bird's-eye perspective of everything around you. You can see what is in the distance, what is below you, what is above you, and what is beyond the horizon. That is exactly what it means to view the larger picture. This way of thinking is critical to your success and living a prosperous life, and will assist you in making sound judgments, making sound decisions, and achieving the results you desire.

The rate of change in today's world is growing all the time. Anyone in a company, from top management to frontline employees, is under tremendous pressure to meet accountabilities while dealing with the reality of today's environment. The problem is that if we work in this mode all of the time, it becomes all too easy to lose sight of the bigger picture.

When you take the time to look at the big picture, whether as a person, a team, or an entire organization, it may create a shift in perspective, adjust your judgment, and eventually change your focus and activities. Taking a big picture view helps to reaffirm what is essential and aids in concentrating your attention on what you consider to be genuine priorities.

You may have heard helpful phrases such as "Take a step back," "Look at the bigger picture," "Think about it in the greater scheme of things," and so on. If you are typically a detail-oriented person, these morsels of advice tend to go in one ear and out the other. They may sometimes feel like a waste of time; after all, why invest time in all that fluffy thinking when there is so much to get done? But what if we told you that scientific study has found a relationship between "big picture thinking" and entrepreneur success? Those entrepreneurs are 30-48% more likely than the rest of us to think in broad terms? (Memon, n.d.).

Big picture thinking is not only important for entrepreneurs, but also for numerous other professional paths, especially if you want to land a desired leadership position. I have gone a long way from being a meticulous person who became irritated whenever something went mildly wrong. It might be being a few minutes late for an assignment, one ingredient missing from a chicken marinade, or a borrowed book that was returned with a dog-eared page (which, for the record, I still do not like, so please stay away from my books).

As I already stated, however, I have gone a long way since then. I try to focus on the broad picture in my big picture vs. little picture strategy, even though the tiny details bog me down at times. However, encouraging large picture thinking is difficult. It requires a lot of effort and mental reminders such as, "How would this affect me in three days, three years, three decades..."

DEVELOPING A "BIG PICTURE" MENTALITY

Ask yourself the following three questions while looking at the broader picture: Why are things going on the way they are? What is truly required? What role do the many single parts in which I am participating have in the big picture? It helps you to recognize areas where you can improve, allows you to convey that big-picture vision to the rest of the team, and reinforces the true rationale for the tasks you undertake daily.

It might be tough to stand back, take a bigger picture view, and analyze the situation when we have pushed in so many directions, with fluctuating priorities and the never-ending demand to generate results today. The alternative, on the other hand, is even worse. You could wake up one day to discover that what once was is no longer relevant, inefficient, or lucrative. While it may appear tough to carve out time in a hectic schedule for big picture thinking, it is important to realize what is possible now and in the future.

I will teach you how to think large and how honing this skill may help you achieve your objectives and feel happier at work and in life. Continue reading to learn six powerful techniques for rapidly seeing the broad picture:

Recognize Patterns That Restrict Your Big-Picture Thinking

Blue sky thinking is frequently thwarted by our innate biases. As a result, the first step is to break harmful habits. Stop trying to be flawless; if you are always fiddling with things to improve them, digging into more and more detail in the process, it is time to take a step back and look for the bigger picture.

Take a deep breath and let it go. If you spend sleepless nights worrying about minor issues in your business, such as where the new plant pot will go in the office, try to calm down and put them aside. In the early stages of a business, some problem-solving is required. A greater emphasis on goal orientation, such as working toward a vision or big picture objective is more likely to result in financial success.

Learn to delegate: If your firm is busy and you have limited time and resources, you may believe that acting on your own is faster and better than working as a team. Unless you are a one-person operation, those who share responsibilities and collaborate are more likely to succeed in their ventures and leave time to step back and think carefully.

If you can overcome these three challenges, you will be well on your way to becoming a big picture thinker.

Expanding Your Perspective

Questioning assists you in connecting the dots between your actions or tasks and your overall aim. "Look at what could be, not simply what is." Asking yourself, "What am I attempting to achieve?" is an excellent place to start, and you should ponder the following large picture issues while doing so:

- Is there anyone else who could be harmed as a result of this?
- Can you conceive of any unexpected effects that may arise if you performed this?
- Are there any ethical considerations to be made?
- How could the concept be used to effect social change?"

Another helpful big-picture thinking advice is to ask yourself, "What am I not asking myself?" Sit with someone trustworthy who challenges you and ask them the questions you are not asking yourself. When your big picture ambitions are in jeopardy, you may also bounce ideas off them.

Think Big by Gazing Up

The chunking approach is a method for producing a big picture. In short, if you are thinking about the big picture, look up and see how expansive something truly is. This is referred to as "inductive reasoning," or "chunking up." When you are not seeing the broader picture, look down into the minute details. This is what is known as "deductive reasoning" or "chunking down." You may also use "abductive reasoning" or "sideways chunking."

Elaborating on this analogy, abducting will lead us to think in innovative, disruptive, chaotic, or crucial ways. Consider transportation as an example of chunking reasoning. You can begin with a vehicle. If you chunk it down, you may end up with the wheel, rim, rubber, tread, and even road. If you chunk it up, you may start with transportation, then travel, then vacation, then wellness, and so on.

Think Big, Then Break it Down

This is a technique I frequently employ myself. Write a bulleted list of the big picture (I refer to them as big picture pillars) and then add sub-bullets to each pillar step. Next, take a step back and consider what you can add or delete from the sub-bullet pointers to keep the needle moving. Bullet points provide graphics for your overall image. It is difficult to connect the dots when you cannot see them. It is also difficult to convey your large image if it is not in front of you. It is critical to see knowledge (in its broadest sense) as a kind of semantic tree; before you go into the leaves/details, make sure you grasp the essential concepts, i.e., the trunk and major branches (the pillar bullets).

Begin Keeping a Mental Map

You can also write or sketch out your plan. When you put your mental babblings on paper, you can quickly see where your strategy is floundering, or how it might be reshaped to match the broader goal. Creating a big picture thinking diary or mind map is effective, and it does not need a lot of time or effort.

To begin, write down your overall vision, followed by the tiny things that are bothering you. The challenge is to ensure that it conveys not only the broad picture, but also the details, or actionable components. You may purposefully draw out zones to ensure that all bases are covered. Then, write down your thoughts to determine whether they depart from your overall strategy.

Take Time to Reflect

Make time in your routine for uninterrupted thinking. This area is critical for making more informed judgments that are based on the larger picture. You will also be able to assess your priorities more accurately, such as what is important in the large picture, how it contributes to the big picture, and so on. This will assist you to quit hustling so hard and get rid of the "shiny object mentality."

STUDYING YOUR OPTIONS

Chances and opportunities might arise when we least expect them. Leaders seek out possibilities for advancement, since that is how success is developed. They learn that if you want to be a success in life, you cannot pass up any opportunity that will help you get there, and that the advantages of seizing chances can help you become a more outstanding person. It promotes your growth and development, assists you in achieving your career aspirations and objectives, teaches you new skills and abilities, increases your financial independence, and increases your access to leadership opportunities.

Once you say yes to an opportunity that calls to you, even if you are afraid or unsure if you are ready, you increase your confidence and evolve as a person. Before you can recognize an opportunity, however, you must first seek it. This may sound obvious, yet many individuals have given up seeking opportunities. This is where the adage, "You would not notice an opportunity if it smacked you in the face," comes from. Opportunities may be there in front of you, but you are blind to them.

Understanding Opportunities

Knowledge is power, and without information, you will not be able to locate the opportunities you deserve. Be inclined to read and explore; everything you have ever desired is only a piece of information away, and the only thing standing between you and a huge fortune is a lack of information. I have been through all of the delays and pitfalls that keep individuals in the middle class, but I was able to overcome them and become wealthy, and I can show you how to accomplish the same using the information I have gained.

You must go for it, even if that means leaving where you are most at ease. Staying with parents after the age of 25 is not a viable option. Opportunities may need relocating out of state, or even across the country. Maybe you even need a new passport to take advantage of this chance. Ultimately, since you may be a large fish in a tiny pond, the opportunity may not be right where you are.

Everything you desire is already in the possession of someone else. Contracts are the same as contacts. What is the size of your power base? What is the size of your pipeline? The more individuals you know, the more possibilities will present themselves to you. Successful network marketers make a lot of money for a reason: they look for prospects that will make them richer and seize every opportunity to do so.

Your next opportunity might be with someone you have never met before. You should go out and meet them. What is the opportunity that you require? Each of these four elements involves work on your part: seeking opportunities, reading and studying, going for it, and building contacts.

Consider the following questions:

- What do I stand to gain from this opportunity?
- Where am I going with this?
- Can I learn from an effective leader?
- Is this really what I want to do?
- Will this chance assist me in attaining financial success?
- Will this chance assist me in getting where I want to go?

Take advantage of the opportunity to network. Do not be afraid to meet new people, as they could hold the key to your success. Take your chance. If the preceding issues have been addressed, do not allow fear to dictate your decisions. You have researched this opportunity, and you know what it entails, so now is the time to take advantage of it.

BUILDING YOUR NETWORK

Whatever field you choose, there will be people who have been in your shoes at some point in the past. It is critical to get to know them, connect with them, comprehend them, and discover who they are. They may be your employers if you work in the industry you want to thrive in, entrepreneurs who have achieved a dream you want to achieve, or someone you know who has gone through what you are going through today.

Unless you do not learn from the first time you do something wrong, you will keep doing it that way in the future. However, that mindset may be improved. After all, why should you learn only from your errors when you may learn from the faults of others? In fact, according to a new study conducted by two academics at Bristol University in England, we may learn even more from the mistakes of others than from our own (Sonnenberg, 2020).

Learning from others necessitates a different strategy than looking inward. As an example, while you may be comfortable acknowledging and learning from errors, others may not be. While most individuals love bragging about their accomplishments, acknowledging their flaws is more difficult.

Approaches for Implementing Valuable Lessons

How can you ensure that a mistake will not happen again once you have determined what caused it? Here are some pointers to help you profit from your own and others' mistakes:

- Learn from the mistakes of others. Several books and podcasts examine the causes and consequences of failure. You can learn a lot from them.
- Do not try to reinvent the wheel. Before embarking on any endeavor, evaluate whether it has been done before and use any lessons gained from it.
- Commemorate learning. Instead of blaming, try to learn. Treat every encounter as a learning opportunity, where errors are allowed, criticism is encouraged, and setbacks are regarded as obstacles instead of bottlenecks.
- Learn from your mistakes and move forward. Do not punish yourself for making a mistake. Everybody is human, as we demonstrate every day.
- Live and let live. Check to see whether a mistake is being repeated. It is okay to make a mistake, but do not let it come back for an encore.
- Make folks feel at ease. When evaluating difficulties, concentrate on the deed rather than the individual.

- Excavate under the surface. Several reasons frequently lead to failure, so do not be impatient and end the conversation after the first reason has been discovered.
- Turn your words into deeds. "An ounce of action is worth a ton of theory," as the adage goes.
- Try not to be too narrow-minded. Learning in one area may frequently be transferred to another. A lesson in athletics, for example, may be transferred to business.
- Improve the learning experience. Strike a balance between reviewing a situation and waiting so long that you forget the facts.
- Keep the lessons you have learned at the forefront of your thoughts. Maintain a journal. While you may recall certain lessons from week to week, many may be forgotten with time.
- If you work in an organization, learning a lesson is not enough; you must also share that knowledge with your co-workers.
- Make a database of knowledge. When employees depart a company, whether via retirement or attrition, they take the important experience with them.
- Create a mechanism for capturing institutional knowledge that others can access in the future.

For example, what are the ten most important lessons you have learned? What are the ten things that only you are aware of but that others should be aware of?

Knowledge should also be shared globally. Create a method for collecting essential lessons and making them easily accessible. For example, ensure that a lesson learned in New Zealand is documented and shared in real-time with a colleague in Belgium.

FIND LIKE-MINDED PEOPLE

Surrounding yourself with individuals who believe in you, in themselves, and their abilities may significantly increase your confidence. Find others who share your interests, whether at business events, online platforms, or in your daily life, as keeping them near to you is another drive that might inspire you to succeed. Many of us can feel like finding others who share our interests is not always simple, and finding individuals who share our objectives and aspirations is even more difficult. Even I feel that way on occasion. While I like and value every one of my friends, there are moments when I wish they shared some of my interests so that we could bond over them.

However, our disparities in professional visions made it difficult to have a meaningful debate in this area. Rather than constructively building on each other's ideas, which only someone with a similar background can accomplish, it is more of a "listen, nod, ask a basic question" routine most of the time. While it may appear difficult to meet like-minded people at times, keep in mind that there are seven billion people on the planet, so there will be at least tens of thousands of people in this community who have a common interest with you.

It is not about meeting a single individual who shares all of your interests, but about exposing yourself to a variety of people who have at least one similar interest. Meeting like-minded individuals does not have to be difficult; it's just a matter of taking the proper steps. Here are some ways you can meet people:

- Clubs and communities
- Online Forums
- The workplace
- People you know
- Networking events
- Seminars
- Social media

Building a Like-Minded Team

We have all been a part of a team at some time in our life. Different responsibilities in the team need the development of talents that a single individual would not be able to develop on their own. One individual may have various abilities but may not be able to perform all of the responsibilities of every function or position. In soccer, for example, the defender may sprint quickly and even score goals, but his or her primary duty is to keep the opposing side from scoring. If he or she is not in the proper place, the team as a whole loses the game. The same is true for every group that is created, especially in the workplace, where the importance of team cohesiveness cannot be overstated.

More contribution and effort from team members toward the overall team goals. Improved communication among team members, ensuring that objectives are met on time. Individuals and the team as a whole being satisfied with their jobs. Better decision-making abilities and increased group engagement as a result of individuals not displaying tension and anxiety when trying to complete tasks. More finished projects and teams in a better position to take on new challenges. All of these are reasons for you to build your team.

Team leaders may employ four steps to create and establish team cohesion, according to Bruce Tuckman, an established researcher in group dynamics. They are as follows:

Forming

When the need to form a team emerges, time should be set out for the team members to get to know one another. Each individual is also informed of his or her expected function, as well as the team's objectives and boundaries. The team leader might use this space to execute team-building activities that help members bond, and also allow for a brief time of grace during which employees could understand the organization's structures and processes. Meetings are held regularly, and open communication is essential.

Storming

Despite being a member of a team, a person may prefer to do their responsibilities alone, rather than with the team. This is especially true for a new team because everyone has a different and preferred method of doing things. It is the team leader's responsibility to make the structures and processes obvious to everyone, reducing misunderstanding and ensuring that everyone is on the same page. Communication lines between team members and the leader should be open and constant.

This allows everyone to express themselves, and when conflicts arise, conflict resolution procedures are used.

Norming

Following a period of resistance, team cohesiveness emerges as team members settle into their positions. Everyone's cooperation and togetherness become simpler and more natural, and individual and collective objectives alike are met with little friction. For this to happen, there should be regular gatherings where individuals may voice their concerns about any obstacles they encounter. It is also a good approach to get everyone on the same page about the team's objectives. The team leader may also encourage activities that are out of the ordinary to maintain team cohesiveness among the members.

Performing

Finally, the team is functioning at full capacity. Everyone should be communicating, trusting, and cooperating, and the team members should recognize the value of working together to achieve their objectives. For this to continue, each team member must believe that his or her worth and efforts are valued by the group. Individual and collective accomplishments should be acknowledged and celebrated by the team leader, who should set new targets for the team to work on while continuing to have regular team meetings for updates.

Emotional intelligence is critical for an organization's success in increasing team cohesiveness. Interpersonal awareness, empathy, self-esteem, fundamental decision-making abilities, mutual respect, motivation, and compassion should all be present. Emotional intelligence allows for the development of norms within a cohesive unit, which contributes to the development of trust, efficiency, and habits among team members.

4

CALCULATING YOUR MOVES

I n the last chapter, we discussed the significance of seizing opportunities that come your way. Opportunities may reappear, so it is critical to assess what you should do next. When you calculate the cost of your opportunities, you are determining whether or not this is a wise move for you. Will this chance make you money, will it cost you additional money, or will it make you nothing? Understanding the expense, you will incur or the benefit you will gain from this chance may tremendously assist you in determining your route to success.

UNDERSTANDING WEALTH ACCUMULATION

Building money is a topic that may elicit intense discussion, encourage bizarre "get-rich-quick" scams, or compel individuals to engage in activities they would never consider otherwise. But is the phrase "three simple methods to generating money" deceptive? The short answer is no. However, while the fundamental stages to wealth creation are simple to grasp, they are considerably more complex to implement. To acquire money over time, you must accomplish three things, which will be described in the next section.

The Three Phases to Wealth Accumulation

Phase 1: Earn Enough Income

This may appear to be a simple step, but it is the most important for people who are just starting out or in transition. Most of us have seen charts that demonstrate how a modest sum saved daily and compounded over time may eventually build up to significant wealth. However, those charts never include the other sides of the tale. Is your income sufficient to allow you to save in the first place?

Keep in mind that there is only so much money you can save. If you have already reduced your expenses to the bone, you should look at ways to boost your income, but are you competent enough at what you do and love it enough to do it for 40 or 50 years and save the money? Earned income and passive income are the two primary forms of income; earned income is generated by what you "do for a living," whereas passive income is generated through investments. Those just starting in their professions or making a professional shift should examine the following four factors when deciding how to earn a living:

- What do you love doing? By doing something you like, you will perform better and be more likely to achieve financially.
- What do you excel at? Examine your strengths and how you might put them to use to make a living.
- What will be profitable? Consider jobs that will allow you to accomplish what you like while still meeting your financial goals.
- How do you get there? Determine the necessary education, skills, and experience to pursue your alternatives.

Considering these factors will set you on the correct track. The key is to keep an open mind and to be proactive, and you should also assess your income position about once a year.

Phase 2: Set Aside Some Amount

You might make enough money to live comfortably, but you do not save enough. What is the problem? The major reason for this is because your desires surpass your finances. Try the following steps to create a budget or get your current budget back on track:

- Keep a spending log for at least a month. You might find it useful to utilize a financial software package to assist you with this. Make a point of categorizing your expenses, as being conscious of how much you spend might sometimes help you curb your spending habits.

- Cut things. Distinguish between your wants and your requirements. Food, shelter, and clothes are obvious requirements, but your less visible needs must also be addressed. For example, you may notice that you have lunch at the same place every day. You may save money by bringing your lunch to work two or more days each week. Adjust to meet your changing needs. As you go forward, you will probably discover that you have over- or under-budgeted a certain item and will need to make adjustments.

- Make your cushion. You never know what is going to happen next, so attempt to save three to six months' worth of spending. This prepares you for financial setbacks, such as job loss or illness.
- Get paired up. Contribute to your company's 401(k) or 403(b) plan and strive to receive the maximum match your employer offers.

The first and most crucial step is to discern between what you truly require and what you just desire. Simple methods to save money include setting your thermostat to turn itself down while you are not home, using normal fuel instead of premium, keeping your tires properly filled, purchasing furniture from a decent thrift store, and learning to cook. This does not imply that you must always be frugal, however. If you are on track to reach your savings objectives, you should be willing to spend in moderation and reward yourself once in a while. You will feel better and be more inspired to work harder.

Phase 3: Invest Your Money Wisely

You are earning enough money or have saved enough, but you are putting it all in safe investments like your bank's normal savings account. Isn't that fine? Wrong! If you want to develop a substantial portfolio, you must accept some risk, which means you must invest in securities. So how can you figure out what degree of exposure is best for you? Begin by assessing your current position. To begin, decide on your return and risk goals. Quantify all of the aspects influencing your financial life, such as household income, time horizon, tax concerns, cash flow or liquidity requirements, and any other characteristics that are specific to you.

Next, establish the best asset allocation strategy for you. Unless you know enough to do it on your own, you will almost certainly need to speak with a financial counselor. Your allocation will very certainly consist of a combination of cash, fixed income, stocks, and alternative assets, and it should be made in accordance with your investment policy statement. Risk-averse investors should bear in mind that equity exposure is required in portfolios to guard against inflation. Furthermore, because they have more time on their side, younger investors may afford to commit a larger portion of their portfolios to stocks than older ones.

Finally, expand your horizons. Diversify your equity and fixed-income holdings across classes and types, and try not to time the market. When one style, such as large-cap growth, underperforms the S&P 500, another may be outperforming it. Diversification removes the element of time from the game. A competent financial advisor can assist you in developing a smart diversification plan.

SPENDING WISELY

Budgeting is pointless, tedious, and most of us never stick to it. Let's make a change and learn how to *not* budget in only minutes per month. Old-school personal finance literature will tell you that if you just make and stick to a budget, all your money issues would be solved in an instant, as if by magic. However, anybody who has attempted budgeting understands that it is a total waste of time.

I never seem to keep up, and I am a financial blogger, so I'm a real nerd when it comes to this stuff. If I cannot keep up with this, I do not expect you to be able to do so either. Monthly budgeting is ineffective because we overestimate our monthly costs. Some expenses, such as accommodation, transportation, utilities, food, and loan payments, must be paid on a monthly basis.

There are also items that you pay for less frequently, such as auto maintenance, house upgrades, excursions and vacations, Christmas gifts, and insurance payments. These less predictable costs may account for only 10% or so of your overall spending. However, for me, they've crept up to around 30% (particularly since becoming a homeowner—home repairs are not cheap).

Accounting for and "pre-spending" every dollar you earn can be a costly financial blunder. If I divide my annual take-home income by 12 and spend that much every month, I will be in big trouble when that unexpected vehicle repair comes along, or when I have to complete my Christmas shopping in December. Consequently, instead of worrying over the comprehensive, track-every-penny budgets that you have always been told are the solution, you should create a basic spending strategy.

What is a Basic Spending Plan?

A basic spending plan is an easy method to the budget that allows you to save money, get out of debt, pay your obligations on time, and yet spend money on things you value, at least within reason.

Automatically track your expenditure and forget about manually keeping track of every beer and burger you consume. The objective is to build up a system that maintains track of all of your spending electronically without requiring any more effort from you, so that you may access it as needed. You may simply do this by using the single-card technique. This is when you use a single debit or credit card for all of your purchases, or as near to all of them as possible, and let technology track them for you.

One of the most beneficial ways technology may assist our wallets is by removing the need to spend cash, and as a result, the necessity to keep track of our monetary expenses. This goes against what many old-school financial gurus say about cash helping you spend less. While this is somewhat true, cash can also be misplaced or stolen, and perhaps more significantly, is slowly on its way out. Whether you like it or not, electronic payments are here to stay, and the days when you need cash for anything over a debit or credit card are dwindling. The nicest part about using a credit or debit card is that it automatically keeps track of all of your purchases.

Determine Your Monthly Expense

Setting up a personal finance app or downloading all of your credit card transactions allows you to do a historical study of where all of your money goes. However, this information is less essential in the long run in comparison to your more consistent payments, and your set monthly costs are what you need to make a priority. Examples of these set costs are your mortgage or rent, payments for utilities, and insurance loans, such as student or auto loans.

It is critical that you first choose how much money you want to save, invest, or utilize to pay off debt. Do the following to find out what is left:

- Total your fixed monthly costs.
- Determine your monthly net (take-home) pay.
- Subtract your expense from your net (take-home) pay.

This is the amount of money you have left to spend, often known as your spending allowance. You may spend it on whatever you want, be it food, gas, alcohol, or travel.

Next, there is the matter of not having any money left over. What do you do now? Take a deep breath; if money is tight, there will not be much left over after you have listed your required monthly costs and what you want to save, if any at all. In the short term, you may reduce your savings objectives while reducing your expenditure, but you cannot eliminate it entirely. Forget about cutting your grocery expenditure by $25. Look for large areas where you may save money, such as:

- Finding a roommate
- Refinancing your home loan
- Increasing your earnings

You may save a little money by cutting small items, but making significant adjustments earns you a lot of money.

Set Your Money to Work for You

This does two wonderful things, the first being assistance in relieving anxiety. It safeguards you from yourself, and you stop wasting time worrying about little matters such as "Did I pay the gas bill this month?". It is more difficult to ruin your finances when your finances are automated, as there will be no more late credit card payments or associated fees and damage to your credit score, and there will be no more missed IRA donations either.

It is hardly rocket science to automate your money, but it is still the greatest method to save more and stress less. If there is one thing I have learned in years of blogging about money, it is that the most essential aspect in financial success is not keeping a budget, avoiding debt diligently, or selecting the proper assets. It is having a system that automatically makes the appropriate financial decisions for you.

Adopt a Spending Allowance

Your spending allowance is the amount of money you have left over after paying your monthly expenditures and saving, and also the amount you can spend each month on whatever you choose without feeling guilty. You can easily keep track of how much of your monthly spending allotment you have used by using whatever technique you have set up for autopilot spend tracking. For example, you might establish a goal in Mint, or use a single card for all of your day-to-day expenditures.

In my personal life, if my family's monthly spending budget is $2,500, I can keep track of our credit card balances throughout the month. If it reaches $2,000 too soon before the end of the month, for example, I know it is time to start shrinking.

IDENTIFYING THE RIGHT INVESTMENTS

When you have mastered saving, investing your money is a fantastic next step, as you may be able to accelerate the growth of your earnings by doing more than merely depositing them in a savings account. However, there are dangers involved, since you may finish up with less money than you started with. The slogan for the popular board game Othello is "A minute to learn... a lifetime to master." That single statement may also be applied to the job of selecting investments; understanding the fundamentals takes little time, but mastering the subtleties can take a lifetime.

Investments are things that you buy or invest your money into in order to make a profit. The majority of individuals pick from four basic categories of investments, which are classified based on the qualities they share. These are referred to as "asset classes":

- Shares include purchasing a stake in a firm.
- Cash consists of money saved in a bank or building society account.
- Property is an investment in a physical structure, whether commercial or residential.
- Fixed interest securities, sometimes known as bonds, are IOUs issued in exchange for lending money to a firm or government.

A portfolio is the collection of assets owned by an investor. As a general rule, diversifying your investments across asset classes reduces the chance of your total portfolio underperforming. Investing may be done in a variety of ways. Many individuals invest in unit trusts, which are communal or "pooled" funds. However, it is also important to consider your own personal values and principles when investing and ensure you stay true to these and invest ethically.

The profit you get from your investments is referred to as the return. Depending on where you deposit your money, you might be rewarded in a variety of ways, for example:

- Dividend payments (from shares)
- Rental (from properties)
- The difference between what you paid and what you sold it for (capital gains or losses)

An immediate access cash account allows you to withdraw money anytime you want and is typically regarded as a safe investment. The same money invested in fixed-income instruments, stocks, or real estate is likely to fluctuate in value, but should increase more in the long run, albeit each is expected to grow at a different rate.

Nobody wants to gamble with their money, but the truth is that there is no such thing as a "no-risk" investment. There is a basic trade-off at the core of investing in which the more risk you take, the more you can get back or lose, and vice versa. However, while you are always accepting some risk when you invest, the amount varies depending on the sort of investment. Money placed in safe deposits, such as savings accounts, has the risk of losing actual value and buying power over time. This is due to the fact that the interest rate paid does not always keep up with growing prices through the process of inflation.

Stock market investments are typically projected to outperform inflation and interest rates over time, but you face the risk of selling at a low price when you need to. This might result in a low return, or even a loss if prices are lower than when you purchased. When you first start investing, it is a smart idea to diversify your risk by investing in a variety of different products and asset types. That way, if one investment does not pan out as planned, you still have others to fall back on.

AVOIDING COMMON INVESTING ERRORS

Mistakes are prevalent when it comes to investing, but some may be easily avoided if you notice them. The biggest mistakes include neglecting to create a long-term strategy, allowing emotion and fear to affect your decisions, and failing to diversify your portfolio. Other common blunders include falling in love with a stock for the wrong reasons and attempting to predict the market. Given the reasons, here are a few common investing errors to be avoided:

Not Comprehending the Investment

Warren Buffett, one of the world's most successful investors, advises against investing in businesses whose business concepts you do not comprehend (Artzberger, 2019). Building a diverse portfolio of exchange-traded funds (ETFs) or mutual funds is the best approach to avoid this. If you do decide to invest in specific stocks, be sure you know everything there is to know about the companies they represent and that this is consistent with your own principles and values.

Having an Obsession with a Company

When we watch a firm we have invested in succeed, it is all too easy to fall in love with it and lose sight of the fact that we acquired the shares as an investment. Remember that you acquired this stock to earn money and consider selling the shares if any of the fundamentals that motivated you to invest in the firm change.

Inability to be Patient

Long-term gains will be higher if you take a gradual and steady approach to portfolio growth. Expecting a portfolio to perform functions other than those for which it was created is a recipe for disaster, which means you should keep your expectations for portfolio growth and returns as realistic as possible.

Excessive Investment Turnover

Another return killer is turnover or moving in and out of positions. Unless you are an institutional investor who can take advantage of low commission rates, transaction expenses may eat you alive, not to mention the short-term tax rates and the opportunity cost of losing out on the long-term profits of other prudent investments.

On a Clock to Get Even

Getting even is merely another technique to ensure that any profit you have made is lost, which indicates you are holding off on selling a loss until it returns to its original cost base. Investors lose in two ways when they fail to recognize a loss. Firstly, they avoid selling a loser, which may continue to fall in value until it is no longer worth anything. Secondly, there is the potential cost of putting those investment funds to greater use.

Allowing Your Emotions to Take Control

The maxim "fear and greed dominate the market" is correct, as emotion is perhaps the number one killer of financial returns. Investing decisions should not be influenced by fear or greed, and they should consider the larger picture instead. Stock market returns can vary dramatically in a short period of time, but in the long run, historical returns for large-cap stocks can average 10% (Artzberger, 2019). Over a lengthy time, horizon, the returns of a portfolio should not depart much from those averages. In reality, patient investors may gain from other investors' irrational judgments.

Making mistakes is a natural part of the investment process. Understanding what they are, when you commit them, and how to prevent them can help you thrive as an investor. To avoid making the aforementioned blunders, create a well-thought-out, methodical plan and stick to it. Set aside some fun money that you are totally willing to lose if you must do something hazardous. If you stick to these rules, you will be well on your way to creating a portfolio that will give you many joyful returns in the long run.

5

FOCUS ON FINANCES

Autonomy is a type of fulfillment and motivation. Entrepreneurs claim that autonomy is the basis of their motivation and yearning for self-sufficiency. To define autonomy, it is to be able to control oneself without having to work for someone else. They run their own businesses, live their own lives, and set their own goals. However, when I am dealing with workshops on financial advising, I tend to first ask them "Why business? What is the motivation?" Many entrepreneurs emphasize the significance of autonomy, or the ability to determine one's own destiny in a company and in life.

Examples of responses from entrepreneurs who took part in a recent session were:

- Tired of working for others.
- Because I am a bad employee, I want to share my important expertise. I want greater control over my job and goals.
- New possibilities and difficulties.
- To make something unique. Bring a concept to life.
- To continue with the '2.30 am concept,' if I did not start, I would not be able to sleep.
- Job safety.
- Independence at home, with family, and at work.
- Fix an issue.
- For a future that allows us to travel, work, and play everywhere on the globe.
- Could not find work and was tired of doing nothing.
- Exciting ideas require an outlet, personal time, retirement money, and a desire to assist others.
- Advantages for you and your family.
- It is gratifying since you get paid for your efforts.
- To accomplish personal/professional objectives.

- To provide high-quality goods or services to people in need.

Some of the responses are motivated by need, such as the individual who started his own business because he could not find work locally and was tired of sitting around. A prevalent theme among aspiring entrepreneurs is a desire for more autonomy in business and life, and the ability to manage their own abilities and skills and control their own fate. Autonomy-driven entrepreneurs must work hard to obtain and retain autonomy; otherwise, the day-to-day demands of a firm and consumers can be detrimental.

Others recognize their own personality type and see that they would make a horrible employee, preferring to manage their own fate and do their own thing. It is also worth noting that some people consider establishing their own business, traditionally seen as a hazardous venture, as providing more job security than working for someone else. Many entrepreneurs are motivated by the prospect of creating a solution to a market problem, pursuing an idea that keeps them awake at 2.30 a.m, achieving goals, and reaping the rewards of both a sense of accomplishment and financial incentives.

The freedom to do what you want, when you want, and even where you want is a powerful motivation. Several of the entrepreneurs in this group were developing internet firms with the intention of running them from anywhere in the globe, with chances to balance family life, travel, and work. Motives for establishing a business are complicated, and motivations other than the classic opportunity-driven vs. necessity-driven difference are more directly connected to business survival and success.

These motives are best categorized in terms of the significance placed on 'autonomy and better work,' 'challenge,' 'financial,' and 'family and legacy' elements. Autonomy is the most essential motivation for entrepreneurs across all business kinds. Many individuals realize they have the knowledge, skills, experience, and desire to pursue a business opportunity, and they can use easily available technology to help make it happen; they do not have to work for someone else, and they can experience a much deeper level of autonomy.

Businesses may thrive whether they were founded out of opportunity or need, as companies motivated by either still both generate jobs, innovate, and export. The most significant determinant for company success was ambition, with businesses that started with big growth aspirations performing the best.

FOUR PRIMARY MOTIVES TO BE SELF-EMPLOYED

As with all business decisions, working for oneself and avoiding a traditional employer is something that requires a belief or end goal in order to motivate taking such a drastic change. Below are major examples of these primary motives, all of which cover emotional, financial, and quality of life reasons for taking such a major step.

- Autonomy and improved work - The value placed on pursuing independence and flexibility, as well as better job prospects, as incentives for starting a business.
- Challenge and opportunity - The value placed on seeking a personal challenge, achieving a vision, and possibilities to apply current skills and receive recognition as incentives to establish a business.
- Financial reasons - The importance of financial stability, increased income, and wealth as motivations for starting a business.
- Family and legacy - The significance of trying to continue or establish a family company as an incentive to start one.

Autonomy is the most significant incentive for entre-preneurs, followed by a challenge and financial motivations. Across all business types, family and legacy considerations were the least important.

Whatever the motive for launching a firm, technological development is simply offering new chances to access customers across the world from rural areas. Technology-enabled new ways to evaluate reactions to new company ideas, known as Minimum Viable Products or MVPs, contact consumers all over the world, collaborate and communicate with others, and outsource tasks.

Technology can be useful. The response to the question "Why begin a business?" is increasingly becoming "Because I can... and because I desire autonomy."

THE TAXES – UTILIZING TAX BREAKS

Being an entrepreneur is a one-of-a-kind experience. You may work from home, establish your own hours, and develop contacts all over the globe. However, if you are accustomed to the 9-to-5 grind and the financials that come with it, you probably have not given much attention to the tax benefits for entrepreneurs. Taxes are quite simple if you are an employee, due to the fact that your company deducts taxes from your paycheck before you ever see it. Therefore, by the time you get your money, you have already paid the government roughly 20% of it. However, if you are a business owner, the tables are turned, as you receive your whole salary and then pay the government.

Here is the good news. Because you deduct taxes from your own salary, you may take advantage of many tax breaks given solely to business owners, allowing you to pay fewer taxes. This means that you can use these tax advantages to decrease the amount you owe before you ever pay taxes. However, are there any tax benefits or tax breaks for business owners and entrepreneurs? In this section, I will show you a few tax breaks for entrepreneurs. Being an entrepreneur has many advantages, especially when it comes to doing your taxes, as they can profit from tax breaks if they know how to take advantage of them. This guide will teach you how to do so in order to pay fewer taxes.

Deduction of Home Office

Deducting a home office is one of the initial tax breaks for businesses. Despite the fact that this tax break receives a lot of attention, many companies fail to take advantage of it. The simple truth is that if you work from home, this is a tax break you should definitely take advantage of. How can you qualify for the tax break? Simply put, you just need to establish a home office, which is a section of your house dedicated entirely to business. Do not be concerned if you conduct business both at home and abroad, as you will be great as long as you utilize your home office substantially and frequently to conduct business.

There are two approaches to be chosen here, those being the simplified and regular options. According to the IRS, the simplified option "can considerably decrease the burden of record-keeping by allowing a qualifying taxpayer to multiply a prescribed rate by the permitted square footage of the office instead of estimating actual expenses." (Chandler, 2018).

When using the standard approach, you can deduct your home office's real expenditures, which may include mortgage interest, insurance, utilities, repairs, and depreciation, according to the IRS. As such, if your home office has a significant amount of deductible costs, the conventional technique will be far more advantageous for you. If your home office is substantial enough, such as utilizing a whole room or a major part of a room, you will benefit from this deduction (Chandler, 2018).

Business Expenditures

Another tax break for entrepreneurs comes from working from home. You can deduct more than just your home office, as your business costs can also be deducted. The difficult aspect is determining what you can deduce, which is when the services of an experienced CPA will come in helpful. Even so, if you are aware of all the available deductions, you will have a better sense of which ones you qualify for. To take full use of this benefit, you will need to conduct some research.

Not every deduction seems clear at first glance. For example, you may be eligible to deduct some entertainment expenditures, such as the cost of transporting a customer to a promotional event, but the IRS does not publicize this information. While there is a lot of information, the convenient sidebar will assist you to traverse the document. You owe it to yourself to do some study on your deductions. You may be amazed how much you might well deduct.

Reduction of Taxable Income

Receiving a tax break merely for saving for retirement sounds too good to be true, but it is not! This one has a few levels to it. To begin, when you contribute to an

IRA, the money is typically not taxed until it is disbursed. This is true for conventional IRA payouts, but qualifying Roth IRA distributions are tax-free. First, however, let's look at the more immediate advantages.

You may be able to deduct your payments to a conventional IRA up to a specific amount if you have one. If you are under the age of 50, you can contribute up to $5,500, and if you are over that age, you can contribute up to $6,500 (Chandler, 2018).

If you exceed those limits, you may be taxed on the excess, so keep that in mind. Please keep in mind that this only applies to conventional IRA contributions, as Roth IRA contributions are not deductible. Again, reading the tiny print is essential to getting the most of this benefit, but it is well worth it. You are not just saving money on your taxes, but also investing in your future.

Deduct Your Out-of-Pocket Health-Care Expenses

When it comes to tax breaks for business owners, this is one of the greatest. You have probably paid a significant portion of your health insurance payments out of pocket, and if so, you may be eligible to deduct them. All types of insurance, including medical, dental, and qualifying long-term care, may be eligible for this benefit. Additionally, you may be able to deduct the expense of insurance for yourself, your spouse, or your dependents.

Have Fun on the Ride

Nobody wants to spend their entire day worrying about taxes. You did not start a business to spend your days totalling up receipts and monitoring the mailbox for IRS letters. By following these suggestions, you will be able to reduce your tax obligation, protect yourself against an audit, and still enjoy the wild ride that is being an entrepreneur.

THE DEBTS

Whether you are borrowing for a degree, a home, a vehicle, or a new business, the ultimate decision of whether your debt is good is the question of whether or not the loans you take out will provide you with more money than you put into them. It appears to be an easy question, yet it may need some critical thinking and analysis to prove its worth. Does taking out the loan still make sense once you take other fees into accounts, such as principal repayment and interest payments? Will you be able to get all of your money back in full, plus the accumulated profit that you deserve? Could you have done better investing all of that time and money into something else?

Thinking in this way will assist you in determining if any debt is more troublesome than useful. There is undoubtedly a case to be made that having no debt is preferable to having bad debt, but borrowing money and incurring debt is the only option for many individuals to finance major purchases, such as a home. This is why things such as credit cards may be considered worthwhile, as avoiding their use can ultimately lock people away from making certain purchases that might be important for their needs. While such types of loans are typically reasonable and give benefit to the individual taking on the debt, there is another end of the spectrum when debt is taken on recklessly. While it is easy to distinguish between these two extremes, certain other debts are more difficult to assess.

The Good Debt

The ancient saying "it takes money to earn money" is often used to illustrate good debt. If the debt you incur helps you create revenue and increase your net worth, then it may be regarded as good and a worthwhile experience. Additionally, if a loan leads to purchases and decisions that ultimately increase your standard of living or improve the lives of your family and loved ones, then you can also consider this a good, beneficial debt. Among the things that are frequently worth incurring debt for are:

- Education – In general, the higher an individual's educational attainment, the better their earning potential. Education has a symbiotic relationship with the workforce and helps to improve your odds of finding an enjoyable career, as better-educated employees are more likely to be employed in well-paying occupations and are more likely to find new ones if the need arises. However, not all degrees are created equal, so it is important to examine both the short-term and long-term possibilities for any subject of study that interests you.

- Business expenses – Borrowing money to establish your own business can also be considered positive debt. Being your own employer may be financially as well as psychologically gratifying, but it can also be very difficult labor. Like paying for college, starting your own business has risks. Many businesses fail, but your chances of success increase if you select a sector in which you are interested and competent.

- Housing & mortgages – There are several methods to profit from real estate. On the residential front, the most basic method is generally to take out a mortgage to buy a property, live in the home for a few decades, and then sell the home for a profit. Meanwhile, you have the flexibility of owning your own property, as well as a variety of possible tax benefits that renters do not have. Residential real estate may also be utilized to create income by renting it out, and commercial real estate can be a source of cash flow and ultimately financial gain if done correctly.

The Bad Debt

Bad debt is what happens when you spend money to invest in an asset that begins to depreciate in value afterwards, leading to nothing but a net loss of income. As a general rule of thumb, if something will not increase in value over time or create revenue, then it is a bad investment, and you should not go into debt to get access to it. Here are some examples of things that you should avoid going into debt over:

- Cars – While it may be hard to live without an automobile, borrowing money to acquire one is not a good financial decision. Cars depreciate in value almost the moment they are turned on for the first time, so when you leave the auto dealership, the vehicle will already be worth less than it was when you bought it. If you need to borrow money to buy a car, search for a loan with no interest rate. You will still be investing a significant amount of money in a depreciating asset, but you will not be paying interest on it.

- Clothes and other consumables – It is commonly stated that clothing is worth less than half of what customers spend for it, but if you look around a thrift store, you will notice that "half" is being generous. Clothes are absolutely necessary for daily life, as are food, furniture, and a variety of other necessities, but borrowing money to buy them with a high-interest credit card is a poor use of debt. Use a credit card for convenience, but be sure you can pay off the entire debt at the end of the month to avoid interest costs. Alternatively, attempt to pay with cash in order to avoid generating any debt at all.

Leverage Debt for Tax Breaks

With so many individuals anxious about retaining their employees and making consumer debt payments, it is no surprise that an increasing number of people are concerned about lowering their debt to reasonable levels. The key to debt reduction is the same as it is for any other diet, that being to reduce your expenditure in the same way that you would reduce calories and exercise more; in this case, you should try to exercise your self-control. The resemblance to a conventional diet plan does not end there, however, as the cure can sometimes be simpler to describe than to implement. However, once you have committed to your objective, there are methods to exploit tax rules to reduce your debts.

The amounts already paid on consumer debt are classified as either tax-deductible or non-deductible. In most cases, mortgage interest is tax-deductible, as is interest paid on student loans and money borrowed to acquire an investment property, such as stocks and mutual funds, up to a certain level. Certain amounts of home equity debt are deductible for tax years previous to 2018. However, starting in 2018, the amount paid on this sort of loan is no longer deductible, unless it is used to buy, construct, or significantly renovate your house. There are also limitations on the amount of debt on which interest can be deducted (Tax, 2021).

It is important to note that credit card and the auto loan interest are not deductible and should be avoided where possible. You should also be mindful of the repayment terms of any debt you already have. Try to prioritize paying off debts with the highest interest rates first, as this will help you save money in the long run. If you have a mortgage, you can consider making extra payments towards the principal amount to pay it off quicker and reduce the repayment amount you pay overall.

Leveraging Debt for Investment

Leverage is the use of borrowed cash as a funding source while investing in order to increase the firm's asset base and earn returns on risk capital. Leverage is an investing technique that involves borrowing money or borrowed capital to raise the possible return on investment. Leverage may also refer to the amount of debt used to fund assets by a company.

Leverage is the use of borrowed capital to fund a venture or endeavor, which leads to debt. As a result, the potential profits from a project are multiplied. Simultaneously, leverage multiplies the potential downside risk if the venture does not pan out. The most common way to utilize debt to invest favorably is to employ leverage to exponentially double your profits.

Here are three ways that debt may make you wealthy through the use of leverage.

Margin Investing

Investing on margin allows you to purchase more shares than you have available funds for. If you have $50,000 in your regular brokerage account, you could leverage your investment and create a margin account, which allows you to deposit up to 50% of the buying price of a stock. You would have $50,000 in cash and another $50,000 loaned to you by your broker. Your $50,000 investment provides you with $100,000 in purchasing power, and you may use this money to purchase $100,000 in shares (Riddix, 2020).

If the stock price rises, you may repay the loan and pocket the profit. The disadvantage is that if your account's equity falls below a particular level, your brokerage company may issue a margin call. If you are unable to pay your margin call due to a lack of cash, your broker may liquidate your whole investment in a stock, leaving you with losses.

Short Selling

Have you ever seen a financial show on TV and heard that it is time to short the market? Short selling is a common technique to gamble against a certain asset by borrowing shares from an investor and selling them with the expectation that the shares will fall in value. Short sellers have made a fortune by correctly timing stock price drops. The disadvantage of short selling is that losses are limitless, meaning that short-sellers might lose considerably more than their initial investment.

Hedge Funds

Hedge funds are among the most active consumers of leverage, being well-known for delivering extraordinary profits through its use. Leverage has been utilized by billionaire hedge fund managers, such as John Paulson, to transform accredited investors into multimillionaires, and many hedge funds have the leverage of up to ten times their entire assets. However, if the fund manager's investment thesis is incorrect, the hedge fund will go out of business, and all investors would lose money. Hedge firms that needed bailouts, such as Long-Term Capital Management (LTCM), were leveraged up to 30 times their assets (Riddix, 2020).

UNDERSTANDING INSURANCE

An entrepreneur exposes himself to significant dangers the moment he begins a firm. A business is in danger even before the first person is recruited, so it is critical to have the appropriate insurance in place. A single lawsuit or catastrophic incident might be enough to destroy a small firm before it even gets off the ground. Fortunately, companies may protect themselves against these risks by choosing from a variety of insurance options. Here are some forms of insurance that a business should put in place as soon as feasible.

Property Insurance

Property insurance is required whether a company owns or leases its premises. In the case of a fire, storm, or theft, this insurance protects your equipment, signs, inventory, and furnishings. Floods and earthquakes, on the other hand, are typically not covered by ordinary property insurance plans. If your location is prone to these problems, consult with your insurer about the cost of special insurance.

Professional Liability Insurance

Professional liability insurance, often known as errors and omissions (E&O) insurance, protects a company from negligence claims resulting from mistakes or failure to perform. There is no such thing as one-size-fits-all professional liability insurance coverage. Each sector has its unique set of problems, which will be addressed in a policy created specifically for a company.

Home-based Businesses

Many professionals start their own small companies from home. Unfortunately, home-based companies are not covered by homeowner's policies in the same way that commercial property insurance is. If you run your business from home, get supplemental insurance to cover your equipment and goods in the case of a catastrophe.

Workers' Compensation Insurance

Workers' compensation insurance should be added to a company's insurance policy after the first employee is recruited. This will cover medical care, disability, and death payments if an employee is hurt or dies as a result of his employment for that company. Slip-and-fall injuries or medical problems, such as carpal tunnel syndrome, might result in a costly claim, even if employees appear to be performing low-risk jobs.

Product Liability Insurance

Product liability insurance is required if your company makes items for general sale. Even a company that takes every precaution to ensure the safety of its products may find itself named in a lawsuit as a result of damage caused by one of its products. Product liability insurance aims to protect a company in this situation, with coverage that may be tailored to a certain type of product.

6

THE ART OF SELF-CONTROL

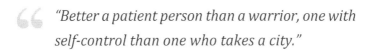 *"Better a patient person than a warrior, one with self-control than one who takes a city."*

— ANONYMOUS

S elf-control is frequently used to define a positive personality attribute in people. The term is widely used, but what precisely is self-control, and why is it important? Self-control is the battleground between impulsive behavior and doing what is good or useful. It is the capacity to control one's emotions, urges, or behaviors in order to attain a larger purpose, like striving to keep one's New Year's Resolution and shed a few pounds. Refusing seconds of supper or dessert later might be tough, but people who practice self-control understand that they are working toward a long-term objective. While the immediate gratification may be satisfying, the long-term effects would most likely be disappointing.

Is self-control really so essential, or is it preferable to live in the now and not worry about the future? A lack of self-control not only jeopardizes one's capacity to attain long-term goals, but also causes additional problems, as people who lack self-control frequently succumb to impulsive actions and emotions. This implies they may make terrible decisions that hurt themselves or others, and they may react negatively when they do not receive what they want.

Consider a child who desires something, but is denied by their parent. Usually, the first impulse is to act rashly, so they may have a temper tantrum, hit, and shout. Children are still learning to control their emotions and behave correctly when they cry. The same may be said for people of various ages. Self-control is a vital skill to cultivate, since these feelings are experienced by everyone who believes that their wants or desires are not being satisfied. A person who lacks self-control, on the other hand, may behave in a variety of ways, including rage, physical aggression, or resorting to harmful coping methods.

When you are ready to take on the world and pursue your ambitions, there are a few skills you should master to get through difficult times and avoid making mistakes. You must exercise self-control, as it will assist you in ignoring urges, controlling your emotions, and learning what to do and when to do it. Self-control is the best method to keep a clear head and make judgments with experience and wisdom while establishing your own business.

So much of success and goal achievement is based on good habits, and good habits are frequently based on discipline, self-control, and the eradication of undesirable behaviors. However, developing healthy habits and gaining self-control is much easier said than done, and it requires a lot of physical and mental discipline to better yourself. Here are a few tips to help you improve your self-control and develop healthy habits.

PRIORITIZATION

Make a to-do list for each day, week, and month, so that when you are feeling overwhelmed, you can see that you are making progress and trying your best. It gives you a sense of control, since feeling overwhelmed and out of control only leads to disorganization, stress, and lost time.

Learning to Manage Stress

Stopping and taking a few deep breaths allows your heart rate to decrease, allowing you to relax in the present. Make an effort to exercise on a regular basis, eat healthily, and get enough sleep, as these all enhance your attention, cognitive performance, and overall wellness. When your blood sugar is low and you are sleep-deprived, you make bad judgments. Exercise improves your sleep and helps you maintain dietary control. Learning how to manage stress in a healthy manner guarantees that you have the energy to keep going when work and life get overwhelming.

Removal of Temptation

We are not designed to continuously reject temptation; according to research, most people fight temptation by removing the temptation, and "training self-control via repeated practice does not result in generalized increases in self-control." (Bridges, 2018). Quit berating yourself for lacking self-control, since we're just not wired for it.

So how do disciplined individuals exist if people are not designed to have self-control? They eliminate temptation, resulting in simple self-control. Rather than fighting to resist temptation, do the same and eliminate it. Set yourself up for success by controlling your environment and avoiding temptations. It assists in making decisions automated and self-reinforcing, allowing you to focus on priorities and decisions that are more important.

Keeping Track of Progress

What is measured becomes managed. According to Psychology Today, monitoring your progress keeps you focused on your goals (Bridges, 2018). Monitoring enables us to become experts on our own behavior, making it easier to regulate and alter behaviors.

Do Not Compare Yourself to Others

You can be anything, but not everything. When we compare ourselves to others, we frequently contrast their greatest characteristics with our average ones. It is the equivalent of being right-handed and attempting to play an instrument with your left hand. Not only do we instinctively desire to be better than them, but the unconscious knowledge that we are not often leads to self-destructive behavior.

Unless you are the finest in the world at something, making comparisons between people is a prescription for unhappiness. Let's face it, only one person can actually be the best at once. Not only are we dissatisfied, but so are others. They are most likely comparing themselves to you; perhaps you are better at networking than they are, and they are envious.

CONTROL YOUR OWN MONEY, AND DON' T GIVE OTHERS CONTROL

You have control over your own fate. Only you can decide what is right for you and what is not. Putting your money in the hands of others might lead to them influencing how you spend it. You have done your homework, analyzed the options, and created your own budget, so you should manage your money the way you see fit. This is a different type of self-control.

Many people put their financial decisions in the hands of others. It is simpler, and we believe they have our best interests at heart. It might be difficult to disregard what the 'financial experts' say, but at the end of the day, you have to live with the choice, and they do not. By educating yourself, you can empower yourself. It only goes to show that, regardless of your financial background, you must still be on top of your own finances. You do not have to be a financial expert, but you should be aware of your objectives and how you intend to achieve them.

Here is a fun story I remembered while writing this. While I was still struggling through my early career days, I had a friend who was known back then for quick success. Maybe it was luck by his side or something else entirely, but he became a rags-to-riches story in an instant. Impressed by him, I stupidly asked him to roll my money for investments and give back returns by keeping a certain percentage of it. At first, he started giving me profit, which seemed far better than I had hoped for. I kept taking the profit he was giving for months without any in-depth inquiries.

The fun part? Well, I got to know after a while that the "certain percent" of what we agreed on was just between us and not even being implied. Turns out I was being given the minutest part of the returns generated, and he was filling his pockets the whole time. Moral of the story? Do not let someone else manage your finances for you.

To begin, ask yourself the following questions: What do you want to do with your money? You may sit down and talk about what you want to do in the next few years and beyond. Do you want to purchase a home? Do you want to start your own business? Do you wish to go on a trip? How are we going to get there? Set realistic objectives based on where you are financially and where you want to be. Take it one step at a time. Focus on establishing a buffer, such as a vacation fund. Build on your successes.

Maintaining Simplicity and Automating Finances

You will not be able to keep up with a sophisticated money management system if you create one that is over-the-top or complex to the point of hindering you. Make your budget or spending plan as realistic as possible. I would also advise you to automate as much as possible. It is not glamorous or thrilling to automate your bill payments and savings, but it works. As we already mentioned in the previous chapter of budgeting, all of these suggestions will assist you in managing your funds.

Start small and automate frequent transfers into your savings account to test it out. Increase the amount you save as you change your budget. Experiment with investing, make a transfer to your IRA, and begin funding your retirement. Keep your system simple and effective by using low-cost index funds.

NEEDS & WANTS

We all know that economics is a social science that studies the functions of production, distribution, and consumption. It ultimately comes down to making decisions on how to allocate finite resources in order to maximize their usage and meet human wants and requirements. We commonly use the phrases needs and desires in economics, but have you ever pondered how they differ?

Needs refer to anything that you must have in order to survive. Wants, on the other hand, are things that are nice to have but are not necessary for living. Every person must understand the difference between necessities and wants in order to spend and save money effectively.

Needs

The term "needs" refers to those things that are absolutely required for a human being to have a healthy existence. Needs can be personal, psychological, cultural, societal, or be other factors, but they are all required for an organism to live. Food, clothes, and shelter were the three fundamental requirements of man in ancient times, but with the passage of time, education and healthcare also became essential, as they increase the quality of life. They are a person's primary priority, since they are what keep us healthy and safe. As a result, if requirements are not met on time, it can lead to sickness, incapability to operate effectively, or even death.

Examples of needs are:

- Safety requirements: a sense of self-security, job security, health security, a safe environment, and so on.
- Need for belonging and love: strong connections and romantic partnerships.
- Esteem Requirements: self-assurance, respect, a good reputation, and so forth.
- Self-actualization: morality, spontaneity, and acceptance.
- Practical needs: food, water, shelter, sleep, etc.

Next, there are a person's secondary needs, which might be anything that is required for one's health or physical condition. For example, if you are fat, you must exercise on a daily basis, since you might not live much longer if you do not have it. If you suffer from asthma, you will require an inhaler. In this approach, needs are determined based on the physical requirements of one's health.

Wants

Wants are described in economics as something that a person would want to have, either now or later. Simply put, wants are the desires that drive business operations to generate the goods and services that the economy requires. They are optional, which means that a human will survive even if they are dissatisfied. Furthermore, desires might differ from person to person, and from time to time.

We all know that human desires are limitless, but the tools to satisfy those desires are finite. As a result, all of an individual's desires cannot be satisfied, and they must seek alternatives.

The wants are something that is very personal to you, whether they are something abstract or tangible. Wants are not always part of your everyday routine, and you can easily live without them. Everyone's wants and needs are not the same, differing from one individual to the next. For example, desires are what you like or enjoy; perhaps you enjoy traveling a lot, which is needless. You will not notice any difference if you do not travel, yet you will not be able to function without it either.

Perhaps you enjoy eating ice cream or sweets, or perhaps you prefer spicy junk food. However, if you quit consuming them, you will be able to live, and it will have no effect on you.

- Determine your fundamental requirements.
- Examine your desires occasionally, since they change based on circumstance.
- Sort the items into highly important, important, and least important.
- Keep track of the costs associated with your goals and requirements.
- Make a budget for a month.
- Spend according to your wants and necessities.

There is a connection between necessities and desires. Needs have a place but wants may be connected to needs. You have the option of determining how your requirements will be met. For example, if you need to exercise, you may do so in a way that you enjoy. For example, perhaps you enjoy jogging, walking, or going to the gym. Your demands can be met in a variety of ways, depending on your preferences. You must be in a state of disarray if you are unaware of your life's many demands and desires. The distinction can lead you to a better lifestyle, but if you do not know the difference, you will squander your time and money on a daily basis.

Decide Between Wants and Needs

Choose wisely between your wants and your necessities, deciding where you must spend money and where you must make sacrifices. Most individuals believe that the only necessities of life are an automobile, a shelter (house), water, and food. Of course, that is a simple task. However, they are unaware of the significance of the time and money they are devoting to their desires.

Always strive to enjoy and cherish what you have, as long as it is yours. Anything may happen. When you want to acquire items you cannot afford, it is simple to appreciate what you already have. What if our goals and needs are diametrically opposed? Actually, it varies and is entirely dependent on each individual's mood and taste. It is usually unneeded for your requirements to be diametrically opposed to your wishes or desires, but the choice is yours. You may transform your necessities into your desires if you so choose. You cannot select your wants, but you can adjust your heart to desire them.

One of the most difficult difficulties of economic growth is recognizing the actual features of want and need and balancing them effectively. When you understand your requirements and desires, you can create a clear picture of how to manage your financial plan. This is a crucial phrase in living a decent life and saving a lot of money.

For example, individuals in their forties and fifties, as well as students working part-time, continue to worry about not having enough money or savings. This is the circumstance or outcome of failing to keep track of and report your spending.

Make a list based on the importance of your life's requirements and desires. It would be beneficial if you recalled that what you have in your life as wishes or wants might be someone else's requirements. For example, it may be that you want to eat whenever you want, but it could also be a necessity for homeless people. Who is in desperate need of it, yet cannot afford to eat it? Your children get adequate vital meals, such as seafood and milk, as well as proteins, but some children may not have these meals; despite their necessities, they cannot afford to eat them.

Routine Desires or Wants

Daily desires are not actually necessary or vital; nevertheless, we are so engrossed in our daily lives that we do not want to consider life without them. In our homes, we utilize desktop computers or iMacs for typing and other tasks. With its position at a satisfying counter, it provides us with a larger screen and a good view. We also utilize laptop computers while we are away from home. This might have become one of our everyday desires, to the extent that we may have gotten hooked. Even if you want to, you may not be able to abandon your regular routine in some situations.

A decade ago, when someone used a smartphone, people regarded it as a mere wish and a waste of money. However, things change with time, and individuals adapt them to their wants, which ultimately become habits, and habits become needs; now, for instance, smartphones have become a necessity for everyone. Consider this for a second: when are you going to be able to utilize the smartphone you are now using? Can you utilize it for the next year, or the next five years?

When technology advances via innovation, outdated technologies are phased out since they are no longer useful and cannot be upgraded to new smart software. This compromise results in the smart machine you are now using. Even if you do not want to, you cannot easily downgrade or delete this from your life, and you have to be a part of this culture. When you plan your life, lifestyle, and work-life, you will establish your requirements and everyday desires.

Understanding Wants and Needs

It is critical in your life to understand what is good and wrong, and it is also important to understand the critical function of understanding needs and desires. It will assist you in adjusting your monthly goals and actively feeding your savings account. There are a lot of things in your life that are just desired. Some items are of high significance in terms of necessities, whereas others are of low relevance. The same is true for desires; many things are just your least significant and least useful desires. If you disregard them, it may be easier to use the same technique for selecting your needs.

For example, owning a car is a must, but upgrading your car to a Mercedes-Benz is a completely unnecessary requirement. As previously said, however, needs differ from person to person. It may be unneeded for the average citizen, but some remarkable people, such as Hollywood stars, musicians, or renowned persons, are expected to have such items in their lives. This might be a case of necessities rather than wants.

Do You Have to Forgo Wants?

This is not the same as removing anything "fun" from your life. It is just a matter of digging through the highland of those things in our lives that we do not require as much as we believed when we wanted to get them, such as decorative items. We have taken them for granted, and are now painfully aware that they never offer the value we previously thought they did.

It is not about giving up all of your goals and compromising to the point that you do not feel good about it, but about making it less so that you can afford a simple yet elegant existence. What will happen if you insist that someone stop using their cell phone? On one hand, they might be able to integrate into society. On the other hand, it might result in a major mistake.

Priorities should be set based on your main aim. Those things in your life that you cherish the most should take some money from your wallet to go to them. Those wanted items might also be your necessities, everyday desires, or recreational activities.

People should save a lot of money for themselves as well. When they need money, whether a small or huge amount, they can use their own savings first in an emergency. The money they save by not spending it on such frivolous items that they only desire can then be used to further improve themselves. Furthermore, by doing this, they avoid having to beg others for money in an emergency.

When you save your money to buy a high-priced Rolex watch, you are essentially transforming your adversary into the most powerful beast. In the same way, when you spend money on brand items and buy them for the sake of showing off, you are feeding the brand mafia. However, if you cease purchasing expensive items only for the sake of wants, you risk breaking the wheel. Stop spending your money on items sold under the guise of an expensive brand when you can get real items from your country's local market at the most inexpensive prices. This will add money to your account, not the accounts of those companies who thrive on your money and interest.

You can save all of your money by spending it wisely. It will take you to the entire tale from the beginning in order for you to understand your goals and require-ments. After that, you will be able to make an informed decision.

PART III

TAKING YOUR WEALTH TO THE NEXT LEVEL

STERLING
PUBLICATIONS

7

BUILDING FROM THE GROUND UP

 *"A business enterprise has two and only two basic functions: marketing and innovation."*

— PETER DRUCKER

Many people commit to starting a business with the hope of achieving financial security. While it is true that getting your business off the ground might require grit and result in some lean times, the ultimate objective of being your own boss is to cultivate financial independence. There is no limit to how profitable your own business may be with drive and hard work, so there is no reason why you cannot attain your objective of accumulating riches.

Starting your own business provides numerous financial advantages compared to working for someone else. First and foremost, you are establishing a business with the potential for expansion, and your wallet increases in tandem with your business. Aside from this, your company is also a significant asset in and of itself. Your company's value rises as it expands, and you can choose to either sell it or keep it and pass it on to your heirs.

Perhaps you have been in the corporate sector for a long time, and are ready to turn over a fresh page after years of reporting to a superior. Starting your own business might provide you with a more flexible lifestyle and schedule, allowing you to avoid feeling trapped on the corporate hamster wheel. Meetings may be scheduled around your family's schedule, or you can work from home. The sky's the limit when you are the boss! You still have to perform the tasks your job demands, but no one is watching over your shoulder to make sure you do it their way and on their schedule.

Starting a business is difficult, and a flexible schedule may not be possible straight away. Even if you work long hours, you know you are doing it for yourself and your family, not for a faraway boss or shareholder.

You set the rules. You are not bound by your boss's standards and procedures or business culture. You may provide a product or service that is in line with your vision. You may even create your own firm based on your own ideas. Maybe you have thought of a method to make procedures run more smoothly. Perhaps you want to ensure that your employees are paid fairly and have adequate family leave. Whatever issues you have faced in the workplace, you now have the opportunity to do something about it.

The pressures of working your way up the corporate ladder are genuine, since you never know if you will get promoted or given the pink slip. These life-changing decisions are made by someone else and are out of your hands.

When you establish your own business, you know you are investing in your future and job security. Furthermore, if you decide to create a family company, you may be able to provide employment for other members of your family as well. Your fate is in your own hands, and there will be no more layoffs in your future. This is likely why many entrepreneurs claim that they never want to work for someone else again once they've experienced the independence of being their own boss and making their own decisions while operating their own business.

Learning to wear a variety of hats is an important part of owning your own business, especially early on. You will need to learn a slew of new skills, from HR to inventory management to customer service. You will quickly become an expert in your field, as well as in a range of new talents you will pick up on the job. You will continue to learn new skills and information as your company grows. You will understand how every detail of your business operates. You will not be able to obtain that type of experience anyplace else.

It is entirely up to you to decide what your company will create, sell, or provide. How exciting! Rather than following in the footsteps of others who came before you, you have the opportunity to create a notion or idea that no one else has ever had. Even if your product or service remains popular, each day as an entrepreneur allows you to uncover fresh, out-of-the-box methods to address problems. Innovation and originality are essential characteristics for a successful entrepreneur, and you will be honing those abilities on a regular basis.

Knowing that each day will offer new difficulties, interesting possibilities, and the opportunity to pursue your passion is reason enough to start your own business. It feels good to know that you have opted to take charge of your own destiny.

MARKETING YOUR BUSINESS EFFECTIVELY

The subtle skill of actively creating your identity is known as branding, but what is its significance? A brand may develop an identity that distinguishes itself from the competitors and strikes a relationship with its audience via creativity, talent, and strategy. Branding is what gives you a name and a future, and because it is so important, businesses and organizations should establish a strong brand from the outset so that it can be constantly maintained as they develop. If you are wondering why branding is essential, ask yourself if there is ever a moment when it is not significant.

Great branding demonstrates to customers what makes you stand out. Assume that your brand is being exposed to a new audience for the first time. Branding that is well-executed has a lot to say, and is able to convey your narrative in an instant. Who precisely are you as a brand? If you do not know, your viewers will not either.

Establish brand-defining keywords and use them to create the company's voice, tone, and style. Every excellent brand should be simply defined by a few keywords. Branding also creates an emotional bond, as establishing yourself as a brand allows you to engage closely with clients, workers, and the broader public. This relationship develops gradually over time, but it begins with building a good reputation, allowing your audience to get to know you, and finally developing unique methods to communicate. Great branding often results from expressing the spirit of your brand in an unexpected way, which takes guts, strategy, intellect, and, at times, danger. Confidence is crucial when telling your customers what makes you "you."

Consider that some of the world's most successful companies got to where they are not because they offered a particularly distinctive product or service, but because of a sense of confidence. Branding offers you a sense of purpose and direction. Whatever your brand is, be sure it has objectives and purpose. Branding is about more than simply your logo, typeface, and colors, as it ties your values to an audience that shares your beliefs. Highly successful companies have well-defined missions, visions, and values. However, this is not just for large corporations and well-meaning nonprofits, as smaller companies might be more relaxed while still creating a core set of brand principles.

Branding can also lead to new avenues. Even the most prestigious brands may occasionally outperform themselves. Rebranding may take various forms, one of which is a logo update. At the end of the day, your brand is a business with a bright future. Part of the significance of branding is that a strong brand is required to achieve the outcomes you want. Branding drives growth, which is why well-known brands generate significant income. Just as your personal identity distinguishes you, your brand identity is the secret sauce that distinguishes you from every other Tom, Dick, and Harry, Inc. on the street.

When you have completed all of your preparations and are ready to begin bringing your business to life, there are a few things you need to accomplish before you can start gaining clients, customers, and so on. Branding is the logo, name of the firm, and visual identity that will attract people. Customers fall in love with brands because they can identify with them; it shows them who you are, what you stand for, and what your objective is. It is critical to provide your potential clients with a well-rounded branding experience.

By developing a brand identity, branding assists in telling your narrative. What are the colors you are using? What is the significance of the colors you have chosen? Does it have any significance for you? Why is the logo designed in this manner? Is there a meaning behind the logo? These are just a few of the questions you should ask yourself in order to realize how significant branding may be. The checklist for branding elements includes the following items:

- Name
- Logo
- Visual identity
- Colors
- Brand vision
- Brand mission
- Brand purpose
- Brand personality

USING SOCIAL MEDIA PLATFORMS

A social media strategy is a list of everything you want to do and hope to accomplish on social media. It directs your activities and informs you if you are successful or failing. The more detailed your strategy, the more effective it will be. Keep it brief and make it as lofty and wide as possible without becoming unachievable or difficult to quantify.

In this section, I will guide you through an eight-step process for developing your own winning social media marketing approach.

What is Social Media Marketing?

Social media marketing is the activity of selling or promoting a brand, product, or service using social media platforms. Social media marketing assists firms by increasing brand recognition, creating active communities, and using native social commerce tools to sell items and services. Social listening may be used to gauge brand sentiment, provide customer support on social media platforms, as well as advertise their products and services to specific audiences.

What is Social Media Strategy?

A social media plan is a document that outlines your social media goals, the strategies you will employ to attain them, and the metrics you will use to track your success. Your social media marketing strategy should also include a list of all of your existing and planned social media accounts, as well as goals for each platform on which you are involved. Finally, a strong social media plan should specify your team's roles and duties, as well as your reporting cadence.

Step 1: Determine social media marketing goals that are aligned with organizational strategy

The first stage in developing a winning plan is defining your objectives and goals, since you cannot assess performance or return on investment (ROI) if you do not have goals. Each of your objectives should be:

- Specific
- Measurable
- Attainable
- Relevant
- Time-bound

The S.M.A.R.T framework will direct your actions and ensure that they result in actual business outcomes. Here is an example: "By the end of the quarter, we will use Twitter for customer assistance and reduce our average response time to under two hours."

Keep track of important indicators. Vanity metrics like the number of followers and likes are easy to measure, but proving their true worth is difficult. Instead, concentrate on metrics like engagement, click-through, and conversion rates. You could also try to track various objectives for multiple networks, or even distinct purposes for each network. Click-throughs, for example, would be measured if you used LinkedIn to generate visitors to your website. If you are using Instagram to raise brand recognition, you might want to keep track of the amount of Instagram Story views. Cost-per-click (CPC) is a typical performance indicator when advertising on Facebook.

Social media objectives should be consistent with your entire marketing objectives, as this makes it easy to demonstrate the worth of your job and gain approval from your supervisor. Begin building your social media marketing strategy by jotting down at least three social media goals.

Step 2: Find out everything you can about your target market

It is critical to understand your audience and what they want to see on social media. This allows you to produce material that they will enjoy, remark on, and share, and it is also essential if you want to convert your social media followers into clients for your company. When it comes to your target clients, you should be aware of aspects such as age, location, average income, typical work title or industry, interests, and so on.

Knowing your fans, followers, and customers as real individuals with actual desires and needs can help you target and engage them on social media. Social media analytics may also give a wealth of information on your followers, including where they reside and how they interact with your business on social media. These insights enable you to fine-tune your approach and target your audience more effectively. Jugnoo, an Uber-like service for auto-rickshaws in India, used Facebook Analytics to discover that 90 percent of their users who recommended other customers were between the ages of 18 and 34, with 65 percent using Android. They then used the data to better target their advertisements, resulting in a 40% reduced cost per referral (Hootsuite, 2021).

Step 3: Research your rivals

Your rivals are almost certainly utilizing social media as well, which means you can learn from what they are doing. Perform a competitive analytical study, as this will enable you to learn who your competitors are and what they do effectively and poorly. You will have a solid idea of what is required in your sector, which can help you define your own social media goals and assist you in identifying opportunities.

Perhaps one of your competitors is strong on Facebook, but has made little effort on Twitter or Instagram. Rather than trying to entice followers away from a dominating player, you could choose to concentrate your efforts on networks where your target population is underserved.

Another method to maintain tabs on your rivals is through social listening. Perform social media searches for the competition's firm name, account handles, and other relevant keywords. Discover what they are saying and what others are saying about them.

Step 4: Conduct a social media audit

Take stock of your efforts so far if you are already utilizing social media. Consider the following questions:

- What works and what does not?
- Who is interacting with you?
- Which social media platforms does your target audience use?
- How does your social media presence stack up against that of your competitors?

Once you have gathered the data, you will be able to start thinking about methods to improve. Your audit should provide you with a clear picture of the objective of each of your social profiles. If the purpose of an account is unclear, consider whether it is worthwhile to maintain it. To help you decide, ask yourself the following questions: Is my intended audience present? If that is the case, how are they utilizing this platform? Can I utilize this account to help me reach my objectives? Asking these difficult questions will keep your plan on track.

Keep an eye out for fake accounts. During the audit, you may come across phony accounts that use your company's name or the names of your goods. These imposters may be detrimental to your brand, not to mention stealing followers that should be yours. Please report them. You may wish to verify your Facebook, Twitter, and Instagram accounts to guarantee that your admirers are dealing with the actual you.

Step 5: Create accounts and update profiles

Choose the networks you want to utilize. You will need to establish your approach for each social network as you determine which ones to use; if you cannot come up with a good goal statement for a certain social media platform, you should consider if it is worth having. Once you have selected which networks to concentrate your efforts on, it is time to build your profiles. Alternatively, you may enhance current ones to make them more aligned with your goal.

Step 6: Look for ideas

While it is critical that your brand be distinctive, you may draw inspiration from other businesses that are successful on social media. Success tales on social media are generally found in the business area of the social network's website, and these case studies can provide useful insights that you can apply to your own social media strategy. Who do you like to follow on social media? What do they do to get people to interact with and share their content? National Geographic, for example, is one of the finest Instagram accounts, mixing amazing images with engaging commentary.

The e-commerce company Shopify is another option, as it promotes itself on Facebook by displaying client testimonials and case studies. Glossier is also a wonderful example of excellent customer service on Twitter. They utilize their 280 characters to respond to queries and solve issues quickly. Take note of how each of these accounts has a distinct voice, tone, and style. This is essential for informing folks about what to expect from your feed, and why should people bother following you in the first place. What do they stand to gain? Consistency also aids in keeping your material on-brand, even if you have a large social media crew.

Social media inspiration can also be provided by customers, so talk and interact with your followers. What are your target consumers discussing online? What information can you glean about their goals and needs? If you already have a social media presence, you might also ask your fans what they want from you. Just make sure you follow through and deliver on what they need.

Step 7: Create a content calendar for social media

Sharing amazing material is vital, but it is also necessary to have a strategy in place for when you will publish information to achieve the most effect. Your social media content plan should also include time spent interacting with the audience.

Your social media content schedule specifies the days and hours when you will publish different sorts of content on each channel. It covers both your daily publishing and social media material, making it the ideal location for organizing all of your social media activity, from image and link sharing to blog articles and videos.

Your calendar also guarantees that your posts are correctly spread out and published at the optimal times to post. Determine the appropriate content mix. Make sure your content strategy and schedule mirror the mission statement you have allocated to each social page so that everything you publish contributes to the achievement of your company goals. You might decide to create a distribution plan along the lines of this:

- Half of your content will bring traffic back to your website.
- 25% of the information will be selected from other sources.
- 20% of content will be dedicated to lead generation, such as newsletter signups, or eBook downloads.
- 5% of your material will be on your company's culture.

Including these various types of posts in your content calendar will help you maintain the appropriate balance. If you are beginning from scratch and do not know what kinds of material to upload, use the 80-20 rule. Your audience should be informed, educated, or entertained in 80 percent of your postings, while 20 percent may directly promote your brand.

Step 8: Review and revise your approach

Your social media plan is a critical document for your company, and you cannot expect to do it right the first time. As you begin to apply your strategy and track your outcomes, you may discover that certain tactics do not work as well as you had hoped, while others perform even better. In addition to the statistics provided by each social network, you can utilize UTM parameters to monitor social visitors as they navigate your website, allowing you to determine which social postings are driving the most traffic to your site.

Re-evaluate, test, and repeat the process. When this data begins to arrive, utilize it to re-evaluate your approach on a frequent basis. This data may also be used to pit different posts, campaigns, and strategies against one another. Constant testing helps you to learn what works and what does not, allowing you to fine-tune your approach in real-time. Surveys may also be used to determine how well your plan is performing. Inquire with your followers, email list, and website visitors about if you are meeting their wants and expectations, and what they would like to see more of, then make sure to follow through on what they say. Social media is a fast-paced environment, and so new networks form all the time while others see demographic changes.

All of this implies that your social media marketing plan should be a dynamic document that you examine and change as necessary. Refer to it frequently to keep on track, but do not be hesitant to update it to reflect new objectives, tools, or plans. When you make changes to your social strategy, make sure to notify everyone on your team and make sure that they all work together to assist your business make the most of its accounts.

THE MARKETING MENTALITY

At its most fundamental core, innovation entails the creation of new products, processes, or business models that better meet the demands of a certain group of customers. However, this concept just scratches the surface of the possibilities of innovation. To understand what it means to be really creative, it is necessary to first debunk some of the typical misconceptions that have formed around the concept of innovation.

Though many people falsely assume that innovation is solely based on inventing something entirely new and original in comparison to the rest of an industry, it can also be argued that another definition of innovation is not how new an idea is, but simply a general notion of time. People often get caught up on the idea that innovation must be inherently tied to something 'new,' whether that takes on the form of a new technology, a new design, or anything else along those lines. Even a next-generation iPhone, which often looks very similar to the previous model, can be seen as innovative in comparison to past versions if it updates the technology even slightly. This focus on the new and modern is undoubtedly a component of innovation, but time can often be more important than everything else when regarding freshness and appeal.

Individuals should be driven to develop their innovation abilities through training, but I recognize that a few characteristics are shared by people who have previously embraced innovation in their lives and organizations. Professionals must be willing to push past the boundaries of expectation in order to create positive changes throughout a company or industry using the power of innovation and new ideas. The ability to think creatively and both absorb and spread new ideas and thought processes from an organization's workforce is crucial for being able to take risks, as well as assisting with hunting down new and exciting prospects in the company's field.

People who are skilled at innovation also have the capacity to focus on a particular subject or topic with extreme levels of depth, using a variety of methods. This can be referred to as being a "T-shaped person", meaning that somebody has both the ability to precisely hone in on a single topic while also possessing a very wide and versatile range of abilities, techniques, and skills. Though not every person is born capable of utilizing these abilities and becoming T-shaped, I believe that these skills can be professionally honed through hands-on experience and exposure to real-world circumstances.

Innovating in the Market

Though it may initially seem hard to act as an innovator in a crowded field or industry, it's actually very possible to kick off and branch out utilizing the right process. Below are a series of steps that can be used as a guideline to help construct an new and innovative thought process.

- Study the competition. Take a look at what your competitors are up to. How have some of their techniques been received by their customers?
- Construct the concept. Getting your team together to brainstorm some fresh and unique ideas may help the creative juices flow.
- Be aware of the possibilities. Having a concept is not the only thing you should do. Where does this concept have the potential to go? How will you bring this concept to life?
- Market. Now that you have researched the industry and your rivals, utilize your new brand and social media sites to spread the word about your new concept.
- Examine the data. What are your consumers' reactions to this concept? Do you need to

evaluate yourself? Do you need to advertise yourself more?

The secret to innovative marketing is ultimately found in the corporate culture, rather than in the products. To begin as a leader and entrepreneur, you may foster a company climate that fosters proactive inventive thinking among your staff. Give them a reason to exist, create the circumstances for them to thrive, then assemble the required resources and abilities and promote teamwork to combine their strengths. Finally, concentrate on the issue. Remember that every excellent concept solves a real consumer need.

8

MULTIPLY YOUR EARNINGS

B y this point, I am hoping you have grasped the financial element of your professional goals. The last element of this process entails reinvesting your profits in order to expand yourself and your companies. However, you still need to multiply your earnings for financial stability.

Luckily, you can start with capital appreciation.

CAPITAL APPRECIATION AND GROWTH

Growth in the market price of an investment is referred to as capital appreciation, and it acts as the difference between an investment's purchase and selling prices. If an investor buys a stock at $10 per share and it increases to $12, the investor has gained $2 in capital appreciation. When the investor sells the shares, the $2 profit is considered a capital gain.

Capital appreciation is the part of an investment in which the increase of the market price surpasses the amount that was paid for the initial investment, which is known as the acquisition price or cost basis. Capital appreciation may occur for a variety of reasons, which naturally depend on factors such as the markets being invested in, and the types of assets being used to fuel said investment. Examples of some types of financial assets that are utilized to develop and fund capital appreciation include:

- Real estate investments.
- Mutual funds, which include a pool of money that can be invested in different assets.
- Exchange-traded funds, or ETFs, exist to track indexes such as the S&P 500.
- Commodities, such as oil and copper.
- Stocks or equities.

Capital gain is only taxable once an investment is sold and the gain becomes realized, and until that point, it cannot be taxed at all. Capital gain tax rates can also vary depending on the amount of time the investment was made, with higher rates resulting from a longer period of time.

However, capital appreciation is not the primary source of investment returns: Dividends are payments given to a corporation's shareholders, acting as a cash reward in exchange for investing in the company's shares. The sum of these values add up to one's total return, which refers to the sum of capital appreciation and dividend returns.

The value of assets can arise for a variety of reasons, such as macroeconomic factors. These factors, which include elements such as strong economic development or Federal Reserve policies like reducing interest rates, encourage more people to take out loans. This, in turn, stimulates the economy by injecting more money into the system.

Stock prices might also rise specifically because the underlying firm is growing faster than any of its competitors, giving it a stronger growth rate than expected by the market and thus making it more valuable to invest in. An example of a stock that tends to fluctuate in this manner is real estate and housing, which might rise due to proximity to projects such as schools or malls that can increase an area's standard of living and land value.

Investing in Capital Growth

Many mutual funds include capital appreciation as a declared investing aim. These funds seek assets that will appreciate in value as a result of higher profits or other fundamental measures. When choosing such investments, it is important to consider whether your choices align with your own principles and values. Growth funds are sometimes referred to as capital appreciation funds since they invest in the stocks of firms that are rapidly growing and gaining value.

Capital Appreciation

An investor puts $10 into a stock that pays a $1 yearly dividend, which results in a 10% dividend yield. After a year, the stock will be worth $15 a share, and the investor gets a $1 dividend. This growth means that the investor receives a $5 return from capital appreciation, since the stock's price increased from its acquisition price of $10 per share to its current market value of $15. When calculated as a percentage, the increase in stock price results in a 50% return on capital appreciation. After all of this calculation, the dividend income return on the stock is $1, which is equal to a 10% return on the initial dividend yield.

For a more real-world example of these principles in action, let's assume that you have recently purchased a home. Capital appreciation states that there is a chance that this house will be worth more than you paid for it in the long run. It is the act of growing value through time. When your assets, such as your home or business, begin to rise in value, you may raise your long-term debt against them and reinvest the proceeds in other ways, such as investing in other businesses, stocks, real estate, and so forth. This can help you diversify your portfolio by adding new investments, profits, and income.

MULTIPLYING YOUR EARNINGS

At some point, you have probably heard about the importance of having multiple income streams active at once, which allows you to have a consistent flow of revenue from a variety of backup sources. However, many people might not realize the number of money-making opportunities they have access to right at this very moment, or why having a wide variety of income sources is necessarily a good thing. The fact you are here now, reading this book, is a sign that you may fall somewhere on the spectrum of indecisiveness. Luckily, this section is aimed at clearing up that miasma of confusion and will hopefully aid you in realizing all the chances for making money that are at your disposal at this very moment.

This is a very basic notion, and you probably do not need an official explanation to understand what it implies, but it's important to ensure that everybody is on the same page in awareness. The crucial advantage of possessing multiple revenue streams is that they allow someone to have a variety of sources that provide a near-constant flow of cash, which puts you in a better position to be prepared if one of those sources happens to fail for any number of reasons. You suddenly have a myriad of options to fall back on in case any sort of crisis ever arises, which gives you a massive increase to your financial stability. In this modern era, the rise of new advancements in technology and the social space of the internet have led to numerous methods of either passively or actively making plenty of money. Before we get into any specifics on these sources, however, it's also important to discuss the advantages and perks that come with having a multitude of income generators.

You probably have a very good notion as to why having more than one revenue source is a good idea, or you can at least guess. However, we still need to analyse them carefully and dig a little deeper.

Earning More Money

The most obvious benefit to having multiple streams of income is that you'll have more money by default. Having a larger supply of disposable income can help you achieve your financial objectives, live a more comfortable life, and quickly pay off any debts you may have accumulated. Consider all of the chances and freedoms that having money pouring in from numerous sources may provide for you and your family but make certain that you keep your lifestyle inflation under control and avoid letting things crash down around you.

Meet Retirement Goals Early

Many people want to retire while they are in their 30s, 40s, or 50s. Of course, you may continue to work on some of your income sources after this point, but getting started on them early can be your ticket to early retirement. Not everyone will have a large salary or make more than six figures in their careers, which may limit their ability to save and invest and delay the point at which they can finally reach retirement. Having several sources of income, on the other hand, can boost your saving and investment rates, allowing you to compound your money faster.

Early retirement is also not contingent on having several streams of income since many people have achieved it with only a paid job. However, extra money-generating streams may definitely assist you in reaching this goal, so it's worthwhile to pursue them anyways.

Diversification

Diversification is the concept of spreading your money in a wide variety of assets and industries in order to give yourself a wider financial coverage, comparable to the old phrase of not putting all your eggs into a single basket. Diversification is perhaps one of the most crucial financial terms to understand and take part in throughout your investment journey, as it is an important technique for investing effectively. Any reasonable investor should want to distribute their money into multiple sources, as it protects the bulk of their income in the event of a single stock or industry crashing during downtime or a bear market. This can also be focused more narrowly, of course; if your focus is on the stock market, then you can spread your assets across a variety of stocks and even real estate investments.

Diversification doesn't just apply to what you invest in, however, but also to how it is you make your income in the first place. Your single day job might be an incredible source of income when compared to others, but there's always the chance that something can go awry and leave you in ruin. As such, it always helps to have other income sources as a backup plan to keep this from hitting you too hard.

Becoming a Millionaire Faster

Before heading into this section, it's important to clarify that this advice will not help you instantly become a millionaire overnight, or at any sort of rapid, accelerated pace. No matter what happens, acquiring that level of wealth takes an incredible amount of effort, and so it's likely to take a considerable amount of time to come to fruition. Despite this harsh fact, having numerous streams of income is something that is absolutely critical to obtaining that high level of prosperity. That constant influx of money will help you reach your goals faster, and with a solid understanding of personal finance and investment practices, it is only a matter of time before you eventually reach that coveted millionaire status.

Having multiple income streams is so important to millionaires, in fact, that the terminology of the "seven streams of income" was coined in order to summarize the most common methods by which they generate their money. In fact, some absurdly wealthy people tend to have even more than these seven, taking diversification to a whole new level. Logically, this approach makes plenty of sense, as having more money constantly flowing in from a wide range of sources increases your net worth and makes you more likely to eventually become a millionaire. In today's rapidly evolving digital era, it is essential to stay ahead of the curve and adapt to new opportunities. As such, the concept of the "seven streams of income" may no longer be as relevant. With this in mind, we have carefully crafted a revised list of seven income streams for you to explore and leverage for your financial success.

1. **Earned Income:** Offer your skills and expertise for income, for example, in areas such as writing, graphic design or consulting. Freelancing is a valuable method to remain your own boss and still earn a steady income. By leveraging platforms like Upwork or Fiverr you can locate clients or consider building your own website to showcase your work. Alternately, you could participate in the gig economy by driving for rideshare services, delivering food, or offering other services through platforms like Uber, Lyft, or DoorDash.

2. **Royalties & Passive income:** Invest in dividend-paying stocks and receive a regular income from the dividend payments. Alternatively, consider creating intellectual property like eBooks, courses, or music that can generate royalties over time.

3. **Rental Income:** If you have the capital and are interested in real estate, consider purchasing a rental property. This can generate a steady income from tenants while potentially appreciating in value over time.

4. **Entrepreneurial Revenue:** Create a Startup or start a small business based on your interests or skills. This could be simply buying and selling such as through an online or e-commerce store to creating a local service business. As your business grows, it could turn into a significant source of income once it begins to turn a profit.

5. **Advertising Revenue:** Ad revenue can be earned by leveraging social media platforms such as YouTube, Instagram, and TikTok. You can earn revenue by creating engaging content and then placing ads on it. The generated income depends on views or clicks and can be increased through engagement and niche targeting.

6. **Commission:** Affiliate Marketing is a way in which you can earn commission by promoting products or services from companies for example on a blog or via social media channels. This allows you to earn a commission for each sale or lead that is generated through your referrals.

7. **Digital Product Revenue:** If you have programming skills or are tech savvy, consider creating an app or software that solves a problem or fills a need in the market. You can generate income through app sales, in-app purchases, advertisements, or even maintenance fees for customers who use your software.

At this point, you should see just how important it is to have various sources of income. It's entirely up to you to decide how many and what varieties of sources you wish to have, as it's not strictly necessary to have all seven of the income streams listed above, but the essential thing to remember is that you should almost always have more than one. If you are someone who is looking towards the future and believes that more financial stability will ultimately be a good thing, then you should try your best to accumulate as many income streams as you can reasonably manage. Three or four is always a good point to start for beginners, but you can always expand further as you grow more experienced and get the hang of things.

Remember that it takes a lot of time and hard work to create a consistent and solid revenue stream, but the long process is also an important learning experience, and taking part in it will help set you on the path to financial prosperity.

REINVESTING PROFITS IN YOUR BUSINESS

Choosing to invest in your company is a thrilling choice. Maybe you had a wonderful year and made new earnings, or maybe you recognized that a procedure in your firm might be enhanced at a fair price. Whatever the situation, you still have the same underlying reason to invest; you want to reinvest earnings in your company so that you might potentially make more in the future. Let's say you have done your soul-searching and have decided on a % or cash number to reinvest in your firm. The true question now is where should you reinvest this money to get the best return?

Marketing: Bringing in New Business

One of the most exciting ways to reinvest in your company is to direct more cash toward marketing initiatives. This has a direct influence on the growth of your firm by bringing in more money, and because you know how much business your present marketing efforts produce, estimating the impact of an increased marketing budget is quite straightforward.

For example, if you presently spend $1,000 per month on a PPC campaign that generates an average of $7,000 in monthly revenue, you may use these figures to evaluate the impact of raising your marketing budget. In this case, if you were to boost your budget by 50%, or $500 each month, you may expect revenue to also be increased by 50%.

Marketing Blunders to Avoid

Make certain that you are evaluating the effect of each specific marketing channel. If word-of-mouth generates half of your income, your marketing spend will have no direct influence on that cohort of revenue. Consider your anticipated increase in revenue to be an upper ceiling, not a guaranteed return. Marketing suffers from oversaturation and low results; as you spend more, the efficiency of your marketing spend will likely decrease. You cannot just continue to double your marketing expenditure and expect to see the same rise in sales.

Hardware: Purchase New Tech

Adopting new technology should be a top priority for your investment decisions. Technology is generally divided into two categories, those being hardware and software. Hardware enhancements might pay for themselves by saving your company time. Because your computer is quicker, you can do more tasks in less time, and you can work more effectively if you have an extra display. From an investing viewpoint, I advocate avoiding purchases that are more about the glitter and instead focusing on those that provide greater value. After all, buying a monitor that is 5" larger but twice the price ultimately sounds wasteful. However, your entrepreneur mentality will be the driving force here, so if that monitor is genuinely worthwhile for your purposes and end goals, then go ahead and make the purchase.

Software: Integrate New Technology Solutions

Upgrades to software can frequently result in a greater return on your reinvestment money. The goal here is to seek software that will help your company function more smoothly, as the proper software setup can save you and your workers hours of work on a weekly basis. It is also priceless to be able to "set and forget" clients, a process which allows you to automatically bill them at set repeated dates for maximum efficiency and minimum hassle.

Another potential alternative is to integrate your existing software, providing your company the opportunity to combine data from many different sources that you already use. Whatever your software preference, be careful when considering the cost, as adopting new software frequently incurs additional expenses in the form of consultants and training.

Increase Retention Through Employee Happiness

Another method you may reinvest in your business is through your workers. The present economy is doing well, and the unemployment rate is nearing historic lows, which means that many of your staff are likely to be contacted with job options and lead to future potential expenditures for your company. Hiring and training both cost time and money, but it is essential to retain good personnel whenever feasible by ensuring that your staff is happy. This may typically be accomplished through two methods: employee benefits and employee growth.

When it comes to employee benefits, go outside the box and give your employees something worth sharing with their friends about, especially if your team is made up of millennials. I have no idea what most of my friends' 401k matches are, but I can tell you which of them have company-sponsored happy hours or bring-your-dog-to-work days. Giving your staff extra attention may be done at a little cost to the firm, but it can save you a lot of money in the long run.

Employee Development: Learn New Skills

Employee development, on the other hand, refers to providing your staff with the tools they need to advance in their professions. It may appear counterintuitive that assisting employees in growing will make them more loyal, but it is similar to the old adage "if you love something, let it go." Giving your workers the skills and training they need to advance in their professions will pay off in a variety of ways.

You will reap the immediate advantage of having a more efficient and informed workforce, but you will also be preparing someone to take on greater leadership responsibilities if and when the time comes. Who would you rather have assisted you in running your business? A brand-new, newly minted MBA off the street, or someone who has been with you for years and understands the business inside and out?

166 | MICHAEL J. THORNTON

There is no one formula for how to reinvest, just as there is no single appropriate dollar amount to reinvest. No one understands your company's needs better than you, its founder and leader.

EMBRACING ABUNDANCE; A FAREWELL

As we draw to the end of our journey along the path of abundance and prosperity, it is time to pause, reflect, and marvel at the wealth of knowledge and insights we have acquired. On this journey, we have attempted to make a comprehensive exploration of the mindset and principles needed to achieve true prosperity. This book outlines the roadmap for you to build a life of abundance, fulfillment, and success. As you stand on the precipice of this new chapter in your life, it is crucial to remember the key takeaways we have learnt and embrace the power they hold to shape your future.

We began initially by delving deep into the mindset of prosperity where we learned that true success transcends material wealth. We also discovered how cultivating an abundant mindset, practicing gratitude, and shifting from scarcity to prosperity form the foundations for a truly prosperous life. By absorbing and hopefully internalizing these concepts, you have begun the process of transforming your perspective and planting the seeds of greatness.

As we ventured into the second part of the book, we focused on forming our foundations for the future. Here, the importance of clarity was heavily emphasized, learning to see the bigger picture, and expanding our horizons. We discovered the significance of calculating our moves, investing wisely, and avoiding common pitfalls. Furthermore, we unlocked the secrets of effective financial management, from leveraging tax breaks to understanding insurance and mastering self-control.

Finally, in the last part of the book, we equipped you with strategies to take your wealth to new heights. Here we explored the power of social media marketing and the marketing mentality as a whole, while also learning how to innovate within the market. We delved into the art of multiplying earnings through capital appreciation, reinvesting profits, and investing in employee development.

With this wealth of knowledge at your disposal, you are now poised to embark on a life-changing journey towards true prosperity. But remember, knowledge alone is not enough; it's vital to put these principles into action and make a conscious effort to implement the lessons learned. As you step into this new chapter of your life, let these seven core principles of prosperity guide your path to abundance and success:

1. **Cultivate a Prosperous Mindset:** Embrace abundance, practice gratitude, and seize opportunities that come your way. Empower yourself and strive for self-improvement.

2. **Focus on Clarity:** Keep sight of the bigger picture and learn from others. Surround yourself with like-minded individuals, fostering growth and development in both your personal and professional life.

3. **Calculate Your Moves:** Carefully plan your financial strategies, budgets, and investments to ensure a sustainable future.

4. **Master Your Finances:** Entrepreneurs value autonomy, taking control of their businesses, lives, and goals. Enjoy the benefits of self-employment, including tax breaks and incentives designed specifically for business owners.

5. **Exercise Self-Control:** Manage your impulses and prioritize your needs and wants. Maintain

control over your finances and resist relinquishing that power to others.

6. **Build from the Ground Up:** Establish a solid foundation for your business, focusing on branding, marketing, and effective strategies to generate revenue.

7. **Multiply Your Earnings:** Diversify your income streams or reinvest to expand your wealth and achieve financial stability.

As you venture forth, the road to prosperity may at times be challenging, but never forget the indomitable spirit that resides within you. Draw strength from the resilience you've demonstrated thus far and allow the wisdom you've gained to guide you through even the most daunting obstacles.

Stay curious, and never stop learning. The world of personal and financial growth is vast and ever-changing, presenting an endless array of opportunities for exploration and discovery. Embrace the spirit of adaptability and remain open to new perspectives and challenges that will deepen your understanding of prosperity and success.

And remember, you are not alone on this journey! Surround yourself with like-minded individuals who share your passion for growth and success. Forge a supportive network that nurtures mutual growth, and together, create a world of abundance that benefits us all. Share your knowledge, experiences, and successes with others, and in turn, draw inspiration and wisdom from their journeys.

As you stand at the threshold of this new chapter in your life, take a deep breath and allow yourself to bask in the radiant glow of possibility. Visualize the life you desire – a life filled with abundance, success, and fulfillment, and recognize that prosperity is not a fixed destination but an ever-evolving state of mind that will continually enrich your life, as long as you remain open to growth and transformation.

In the pursuit of prosperity, remember that the journey itself is just as important as the destination. Cherish each step along the way and allow yourself to grow and evolve through every triumph and setback. Embrace the process with gratitude, for it is through these experiences that we gain the wisdom and resilience needed to thrive in a world of ever-changing circumstances.

In closing, know that you are now equipped with the tools, principles, and mindset necessary to create a life of true prosperity. Your dreams and aspirations are no longer mere fantasies but tangible goals that can be realized through dedication, hard work, and the application of the knowledge you've gained. Be bold, be courageous, and take the first step towards a brighter, more prosperous future.

May the path before you be illuminated with the light of wisdom and the warmth of success. May you find joy and fulfillment in your journey towards true prosperity, and may your life be a shining example of the power and potential that lies within each of us. Embrace the principles of abundance and create a life that resonates with the deepest desires of your heart.

If this book has touched your life or inspired you to reach for greater heights, we encourage you to share your thoughts and experiences with others. Please consider leaving a review on Amazon, as your feedback not only helps the author but also serves as a beacon of inspiration for others seeking to transform their lives.

Thank you for embarking on this journey with us, and may you find prosperity, success, and fulfillment in all aspects of your life.

REFERENCES

Artzberger, W. (2019). *Avoid These 8 Common Investing Mistakes.* Investopedia. https://www.investopedia.com/articles/stocks/07/beat_the_mistakes.asp

Bridges, F. (2018, June 28). *5 Ways To Improve Self-Control.* Forbes. https://www.forbes.com/sites/francesbridges/2018/06/28/5-ways-to-improve-self-control/?sh=70ee889a21d5

Castrillon, C. (2020, August 12). *5 Ways To Go From A Scarcity To Abundance Mindset.* Forbes. https://www.forbes.com/sites/carolinecastrillon/2020/07/12/5-ways-to-go-from-a-scarcity-to-abundance-mindset/?sh=5facda701197

Chandler, I. (2018, August 28). *The 6 Best Tax Advantages To Being An Entrepreneur - WealthFit.* Https://Wealthfit.com. https://wealthfit.com/articles/tax-advantages-of-being-an-entrepreneur/

Chen, J. (2020). *Capital Appreciation.* Investopedia. https://www.investopedia.com/terms/c/capitalappreciation.asp

Dixon, A. (2020, May 29). *Survey: 1 In 5 Working Americans Aren't Saving Anything At All | Bankrate.com.* Bankrate. https://www.bankrate.com/banking/savings/financial-security-march-2019/

Esplin, B. (2016, March 10). *Money Funnies: 15 Humorous Money Quotes and the Serious Lessons they Teach.* The Micawber Principle. http://micawberprinciple.com/money-funnies-15-humorous-money-quotes-and-the-serious-lessons-they-teach-1257/

Hootsuite. (2021, May 14). *How to Create a Social Media Marketing Strategy in 8 Easy Steps.* Hootsuite Social Media Management. https://blog.hootsuite.com/how-to-create-a-social-media-marketing-plan/

Memon, M. (n.d.). *6 ways to develop big picture thinking (and stop drowning in detail).* Www.fingerprintforsuccess.com. Retrieved July 10, 2021, from https://www.fingerprintforsuccess.com/blog/big-picture-thinking

Mumford, K. J. (2016). Prosperity, Sustainability and the Measurement of Wealth. *Asia & the Pacific Policy Studies*, 3(2), 226–234. https://doi.org/10.1002/app5.132

Riddix, M. (2020, October 23). *5 Ways Debt Can Make You Money*. Investopedia. https://www.investopedia.com/financial-edge/0710/5-ways-debt-can-make-you-money.aspx

Sonnenberg, F. (2020, August 11). *How to Learn from the Mistakes of Other People — Frank Sonnenberg*. Frank Sonnenberg Online. https://www.franksonnenbergonline.com/blog/how-to-learn-from-the-mistakes-of-other-people/

Tax, T.-T., Income. (2021, May 3). *Taxes and Reducing Debt*. Turbotax.intuit.com. https://turbotax.intuit.com/tax-tips/debt/taxes-and-reducing-debt/L7qfzotzX

Tellum, B. (2018, December 30). *Team Cohesion: Collaboration of Like-Minded Individuals to Perform*. The Minded Athlete. https://themindedathlete.com/team-cohesion/

Printed in Great Britain
by Amazon

22102430R00099